The Biography of the Last French King, Revolution and the Fall of the Monarchy

By United Library

https://campsite.bio/unitedlibrary

Table of Contents

Table of Contents 2

Disclaimer 4

Introduction 5

Louis XVI 6

Birth, Undressing and Baptism... 10

Youth and preparation for power (1754-1774) 13

Heir to the crown of France 18

King of France and Navarre (1774-1791) 34

Coronation ceremony... 41

Beginnings of the Revolution 88

King of the French and monarchy (1791-1792) 125

Abolition of the monarchy and last months (1792-1793).....135

Tributes 146

Other books by United Library.. 157

Disclaimer

This biography book is a work of nonfiction based on the public life of a famous person. The author has used publicly available information to create this work. While the author has thoroughly researched the subject and attempted to depict it accurately, it is not meant to be an exhaustive study of the subject. The views expressed in this book are those of the author alone and do not necessarily reflect those of any organization associated with the subject. This book should not be taken as an endorsement, legal advice, or any other form of professional advice. This book was written for entertainment purposes only.

Introduction

Louis XVI was a French king born in 1754, who succeeded his grandfather Louis XV and ascended the throne at age 20. His rule was marked by attempts to reform the government according to Enlightenment ideals, which were met with hostility from the French nobility.

He implemented deregulation of grain prices, supported American colonists' independence from Great Britain, and attempted to reduce taxation on serfs and workers. Louis XVI's indecision caused unrest among members of lower classes, prompting events like the storming of the Bastille which resulted in him recognizing legislative authority over himself. With rebellion spreading through France, Louis XVI unsuccessfully attempted to flee but ended up captured and tried for high treason.

He was executed on 21 January 1793 by guillotine as a desacralized citizen under the name Citizen Louis Capet. His death brought an end to more than a thousand years of continuous monarchy in France; both his sons died before they reached adulthood while his only surviving child Marie Thérèse eventually passed away without children in 1851.

Louis XVI

Louis XVI, born on August 23, 1754 in Versailles under the name of Louis-Auguste de France and died on January 21, 1793 in Paris, was king of France and Navarre from May 10, 1774 to November 6, 1789, then king of France until September 21, 1792. He is the last king of France of the period called the Ancien Régime.

Son of the dauphin Louis of France and Marie-Josèphe of Saxony, he became dauphin at the death of his father. Married in 1770 to Marie-Antoinette of Austria, he ascended the throne in 1774, at the age of nineteen, upon the death of his grandfather Louis XV.

Inheriting a kingdom on the verge of bankruptcy, he launched several financial reforms, notably carried out by the ministers Turgot, Calonne and Necker, such as the project of a direct egalitarian tax, but all of them failed in the face of the blocking of the parliaments, the clergy, the nobility and the court. He made changes in the law of persons (abolition of torture, serfdom, etc.) and won a great military victory against England, through his active support to the American independence fighters. But the French intervention in America ended up ruining the kingdom.

Louis XVI is mainly known for his role in the French Revolution. It began in 1789 after the convocation of the Estates General to refinance the state. The deputies of the Third, who claimed the support of the people, proclaimed themselves "National Assembly" and put a *de facto* end to the absolute monarchy of divine right. At first, Louis XVI had to leave the Palace of Versailles - he was the last monarch to live there - for Paris, and seemed to accept to become a constitutional monarch. But before the promulgation of the Constitution of 1791, the royal family left the capital and was arrested in Varennes. The failure of this escape had a significant impact on public opinion, which until then had not been very hostile to the sovereign, and marked a fracture among the conventioneers.

Having become a constitutional king, Louis XVI appointed and governed with several ministries, first the feuillant and then the girondin. He actively contributed to the outbreak of a war between the absolute monarchies and the revolutionaries, in April 1792. The progression of foreign and monarchist armies towards Paris provoked, during the day of August 10, 1792, his overthrow by the republican sections, then the abolition of the monarchy the following month. Imprisoned and then judged guilty of intelligence with the enemy, the one called by the revolutionaries "Louis Capet" was condemned to death and guillotined on the Place de la Révolution in Paris. The queen and the king's sister Elisabeth met the same fate a few months later.

Nevertheless, royalty did not disappear with him: after having gone into exile, his two younger brothers reigned over France under the names of Louis XVIII and Charles X, between 1814 and 1830. The son of Louis XVI, imprisoned in the Temple prison, had been recognized as king of France under the name of "Louis XVII" by the monarchists, before dying in his jail in 1795, without ever having reigned.

After initially considering him either as a traitor to the fatherland or as a martyr, French historians generally adopt a nuanced view of the personality and role of Louis XVI, generally agreeing that his character was not up to the exceptional circumstances of the revolutionary period.

Veuë du Chasteau de Versaille du côté du Partorre d'Eau

Birth, Undressing and Baptism

Louis-Auguste de France was born at the Palace of Versailles on August 23, 1754 at 6:24 am.

He was the fifth child and third son of the dauphin Louis of France (1729-1765), the fourth with his second wife Marie-Josèphe of Saxony. From the union of this couple were born a total of eight children:

1. Marie-Zéphyrine of France (1750-1755) ;

2. Louis of France (1751-1761), Duke of Burgundy;

3. Xavier de France (1753-1754), Duke of Aquitaine;

4. Louis-Auguste de France, duke of Berry, future Louis XVI;

5. Louis Stanislas Xavier of France (1755-1824), Count of Provence, who became king under the name of *Louis XVIII* in 1814 (recognized as such after the death of Louis XVII in 1795 by certain European powers);

6. Charles Philippe de France (1757-1836), count of Artois, who became king under the name of *Charles X* at the death of the previous king;

7. Clotilde de France (1759-1802), queen of Sardinia from 1796 to 1802 by her marriage to King Charles-Emmanuel IV of Sardinia;

8. Elisabeth of France (1764-1794), she shared the fate of the royal family until the last moments. She was guillotined.

From a first marriage with Maria Theresa of Spain, Louis had a daughter Maria Theresa of France (1746-1748).

Many people were there to witness the arrival of the newborn: the royal family's midwife Jard, the chancellor Guillaume de Lamoignon de Blancmesnil, the keeper of the seals Jean-Baptiste de Machault d'Arnouville and the general controller of finances Jean Moreau de Séchelles, porters, bodyguards and the sentry. The dauphin, in his robe, welcomes everyone saying: "Come in, my friend, come in quickly, to see my wife give birth."

Shortly before the birth, Binet, the dauphin's first valet, sent a pikeman from the Petite Écurie to tell Louis XV, the grandfather of the future baby, of the impending birth, while the king was in his summer quarters at the Château de Choisy-le-Roi. Just after the birth, the dauphin sent one of his squires, M. de Montfaucon, to announce the birth itself. On the road, Montfaucon crossed the pikeman who, having fallen off his horse and died shortly afterwards, had not been able to carry the first message. The squire brought both messages to the king at the same time: the one about the birth *to come* and the one about the birth *that had taken place*. Thus informed, Louis XV gave 10 louis to the pikeman and 1 000 livres to the squire before going immediately to Versailles.

Immediately after his birth, the baby is undone in the church of Notre-Dame de Versailles by Sylvain-Léonard de Chabannes (1718-1812), chaplain to the king.

When the king entered the room, he seized the newborn and named him *Louis-Auguste* before immediately naming him Duke of Berry. The baby was immediately entrusted to the countess of Marsan, governess of the children of France, before being taken to his apartment by Louis François Anne de Neufville de Villeroy, duke of Villeroy and captain of the king's bodyguards

The news of the birth was announced to the European sovereigns allied with the crown as well as to Pope Benedict XIV. Around 1:00 pm, the king and Queen Marie Leszczyńska attend a *Te Deum in the* castle chapel. The bells of the churches of Paris begin to ring and, in the evening, a fireworks display is fired from the Place d'Armes and lit by the king's hand with a "running rocket" from his balcony.

Youth and preparation for power (1754-1774)

In the shadow of the Duke of Burgundy

The newborn suffers from a rather fragile health during the first months of its life. It is said that he has a "weak and valetudinous temperament". His nurse, who was also the mistress of the Marquis de La Vrillière, did not give enough milk. At the insistence of the Dauphine, she is replaced by Madame Mallard. From May 17 to September 27, 1756, the Duke of Berry and his elder brother, the Duke of Burgundy, were sent to the castle of Bellevue on the advice of the Genevan doctor Theodore Tronchin, in order to breathe healthier air than at Versailles.

Like his brothers, the Duke of Berry had the Countess of Marsan as his governess, the governess of the royal children. The latter favored, on the one hand, the Duke of Burgundy as heir to the throne, and on the other hand the Count of Provence, whom she preferred to his brothers. Feeling neglected, the duke of Berry will never really carry her in his heart and, once crowned king, he will always refuse to attend the parties that she organized for the royal family. The governess was in charge of teaching the children to read, write and study history. Their parents closely supervised this education, with the dauphine teaching them the history of religions and the dauphin languages and morals. He taught them that "all men are equal by right of nature and in the eyes of God who created them.

As the king's grandson, the duke of Berry was bound, like his brothers, to a certain number of obligations and rituals: they attended both royal funerals (which were not lacking between 1759 and 1768) and the marriages of important figures of the court, and they were obliged to welcome foreign sovereigns and men of the Church in particular, in spite of their young age. Thus, in May 1756, three new cardinals visited them: "Burgundy (5 years old) received them, listened to their speeches and harangued them, while Berry (22 months old) and Provence (6 months old), gravely seated on armchairs, with their robes and their little caps, imitated the gestures of their elders.

As they grew up, the king's grandsons had to move from the skirts of their governess to the hands of a governor in charge of all educational activities. After having thought of the Count of Mirabeau (father of the future revolutionary), the dauphin chose for his children in 1758 a man closer to monarchical ideas: the Duke of La Vauguyon, Prince of Carency and peer of France. The latter called his pupils the "*Four Fs*": *the Fine* (Duke of

Burgundy), *the Weak* (Duke of Berry), *the False* (Count of Provence) and *the Frank* (Count of Artois). La Vauguyon was assisted by four deputies: Jean-Gilles du Coëtlosquet (preceptor), André-Louis-Esprit de Sinéty de Puylon (sub-governor), Claude-François Lizarde de Radonvilliers (sub-preceptor) and Jean-Baptiste du Plessis d'Argentré (reader). The dauphin asked La Vauguyon to base himself on the Holy Scriptures and the model of Idomeneus, the hero of Fénelon's *Telemachus*: "You will find in it all that is appropriate for the direction of a king who wants to fulfill perfectly all the duties of royalty. This last aspect is privileged because the future Louis XVI (and his younger brothers), not being destined to wear the crown, is kept away from business, he is not taught to govern.

It was the custom of the court that the royal children passed from their governess to the governor at the age of seven. Thus the Duke of Burgundy was handed over to the Duke of La Vauguyon on 1er May 1758, shortly before his seventh birthday, thus leaving the child's robes for the male clothes. This separation from his governess is difficult for her as well as for him, and the duke of Berry is also saddened by this sudden separation. The duke of Burgundy is admired by his parents and by the court. Intelligent and sure of himself, he remains capricious and convinced of his superiority. One day he questions his relatives saying "Why wasn't I born God?" Everything seems to show that he will be a great king.

An insignificant event will change the destiny of the royal family: in the spring of 1760, the Duke of Burgundy falls from a cardboard horse that he had been given some time earlier. He began to limp and the doctors discovered a lump on his hip. The operation he underwent did nothing. The prince was then condemned to stay in his room and his studies were interrupted. He wished to be consoled by his little brother, the Duke of Berry. Thus, in 1760, the future king exceptionally passed into the hands of the governor before reaching the age of 7. La Vauguyon recruited a second sub-preceptor for him. The two brothers were then educated together, the Duke of Burgundy entertaining himself by collaborating in the education of his younger brother, and the latter being more interested in geography and mechanical arts. The health of the Duke of Burgundy worsens nevertheless and in November 1760 he is diagnosed with a double tuberculosis (pulmonary and bone). The court had to face the facts: the death of the prince was as imminent as it was inevitable. His parents are in "an overwhelming pain that we can not imagine. In the emergency, the child is baptized on November 29, 1760, makes his first communion the next day and receives the extreme unction on March 16, 1761 before dying in odor of sanctity on March 22 following, in the absence of his grand-brother, also bedridden by a high fever.

Heir to the crown of France

The death of the Duke of Burgundy was experienced as a tragedy for the dauphin and the dauphine. The latter will declare: "nothing can tear from my heart the pain which is engraved there forever". One installs the duke of Berry in the apartments of his big brother.

On October 18, 1761, the same day as his brother Louis Stanislas Xavier, Louis Auguste was baptized by Archbishop Charles Antoine de La Roche-Aymon in the royal chapel of the Palace of Versailles, in the presence of Jean-François Allart (1712-1775), the parish priest of the church of Notre-Dame de Versailles. His godfather was his grandfather Auguste III of Poland, represented by Louis-Philippe, Duke of Orleans, and his godmother was Marie Adélaïde of France.

Louis-Auguste was already distinguished by a great shyness; some saw this as a lack of character, as did the Duc de Croÿ in 1762: "We noticed that of the three Children of France, there was only Monsieur de Provence who showed spirit and a resolute tone. Monsieur de Berry, who was the eldest and the only one in the hands of men, seemed to be very stiff. Nevertheless, he sometimes showed himself at ease in front of the historians and philosophers who came to the court. He also shows humour and repartee. La Vauguyon and the preacher Charles Frey de Neuville even notice in the young man enough great qualities to make him a good king.

Intellectually, Berry is a gifted and conscientious student. He excels in the following subjects : geography, physics, writing, morals, public law, history, dance, drawing, fencing, religion and mathematics. He learned several languages (Latin, German, Italian and English) and enjoyed some of the great classics of literature such as *La Jérusalem délivrée*, *Robinson Crusoe* and *Athalie* by Jean Racine. His father was nevertheless intransigent and sometimes deprived him of hunting at the slightest slackening. A studious student, he was passionate about several scientific disciplines. According to the French historian Ran Halévi: "Louis XVI received the education of a "prince of the Enlightenment" - He was an enlightened monarch. History professors Philippe Bleuzé and Muriel Rzeszutek state that: "Louis XVI knew Latin, German, Spanish, mastered English perfectly, practiced logic, grammar, rhetoric, geometry, astronomy. He had an undeniable historical and geographical culture and skills in economics". They believe that "he was very influenced by Montesquieu, who inspired him with a modern conception of monarchy detached from divine right".

The destiny of the duke of Berry was to be turned upside down again by an insignificant event. On August 11, 1765, the dauphin, his father, made a visit to the abbey of Royallieu and returned to Versailles in the rain. Already in poor health and suffering from a cold, he was taken by a violent fever. He managed to have the court transported to the castle of Fontainebleau for a change of air, but nothing was done and his condition worsened over the months. After an agony of 35 days, the dauphin died on December 20, 1765 at the age of 36.

At the death of his father, the duke of Berry became dauphin of France. He was 11 years old and had the vocation to succeed immediately to the king, his grandfather, who was 56.

End of education

Louis-Auguste is now dauphin, but this change of status does not exempt him from continuing his education, on the contrary. La Vauguyon recruited an additional assistant to teach the dauphin morals and public law: Father Guillaume François Berthier. The governor encouraged the duke of Berry to think for himself by applying the method of free examination. To do this, he asked him to write eighteen moral and political maxims; the dauphin did this effectively and managed to advocate, among other things, free trade, the rewarding of citizens, and the moral example that the king should set (a thinly veiled allusion to the antics of Louis XV). The work was rewarded by La Vauguyon, who even had it printed. The dauphin even wrote a book in which the ideas inspired by his governor were recounted: *Réflexions sur mes Entretiens avec M. le duc de La Vauguyon (Reflections on my Talks with the Duke of La Vauguyon)*; in it, he forged his vision of the monarchy by stating, for example, that the kings themselves "are responsible for all the injustices that they have not been able to prevent". His mother tempered this liberal impulse by inculcating in him the precepts of the Catholic religion; thus the dauphin received the sacrament of confirmation on December 21, 1766 and made his first communion the following December 24. As he grew up, Berry started to go out more and practiced horseback riding. He also begins to have a passion for clock making and locksmithing, two hobbies that will never leave him. The abbot Jacques-Antoine Soldini comes to reinforce the religious education of the young man.

The education of the dauphin will stop with his "establishment", that is his marriage. This was celebrated in Versailles on May 16, 1770 with the young Marie-Antoinette of Austria. On this occasion, the abbot Soldini addressed to the dauphin a long letter of advice and recommendations for his life to come, and in particular on the "bad readings" to be avoided and on the attention to be paid to his diet. Finally, he exhorted him to always remain punctual, kind, affable, frank, open but careful in his words. Soldini would later become the confessor of the dauphin who became king.

Marriage with Marie-Antoinette of Austria

The marriage of the Dauphin was considered in 1766 by Étienne-François de Choiseul when the future king was only 12 years old. The kingdom of France had been weakened by the Seven Years' War, and the Secretary of State thought it wise to ally with Austria against the powerful kingdom of Great Britain. The king was convinced of the project, and on May 24, 1766, the Austrian ambassador in Paris wrote to the Archduchess Marie-Thérèse that she "can from this moment consider as decided and assured the marriage of the dauphin and the Archduchess Marie-Antoinette. The mother of the dauphin makes nevertheless suspend the project with the aim of maintaining the court of Vienna in the expectation, "between the fear and the hope". "To suspend" is the appropriate term, because she dies a few months later, on March 13, 1767. The project of marriage is then put back on the table.

Shortly after the death of Marie-Josèphe de Saxe, the Marquis de Durfort was sent on a mission to Vienna to convince the archduchess and her son of the political benefits of this union. The negotiations lasted several years, and the image given by the dauphin was not always brilliant: Florimond de Mercy-Argenteau, the Austrian ambassador in Paris, points out to him that "nature seems to have refused any gift to Mr. the Dauphin, [...], by its content and its remarks this prince announces only a very limited sense, much disgrace and null sensitivity". In spite of these opinions, and in spite of the young age of the interested parties (15 years for Louis-Auguste and 14 for Marie-Antoinette), the empress sees in this marriage the interest of her country and gives her agreement. On April 17, 1770, Marie-Antoinette officially renounced the succession to the Austrian throne and on April 19, a wedding ceremony was held in Vienna, with the Marquis de Durfort signing the marriage certificate on behalf of the Dauphin.

Marie-Antoinette left for France on April 21, 1770 during a journey that lasted more than 20 days accompanied by a procession of about 40 vehicles. The procession arrived in Strasbourg on May 7. The ceremony of "handing over the bride" will take place in the middle of the Rhine, at equal distance between the two banks, on the "Île aux Epis". In a pavilion built on this islet, the young woman exchanged her Austrian clothes for French ones, before going back across the Rhine, to a French procession and next to the countess of Noailles, her new lady-in-waiting. The meeting between the dauphin and his future wife took place on May 14, 1770, at the bridge of Berne, in the forest of Compiègne. The king, the dauphin and the court were there to welcome the procession. When she got out of the carriage, the future dauphin curtsied to the king and was presented by him to the duke of Berry, who gave her a discreet kiss on the cheek. The royal carriage then took the king, the dauphin and his future wife to the castle of Compiègne, where an official reception was held that evening to introduce the future dauphin to the principal members of the court. The next day, the procession stopped at the Carmelite monastery of Saint-Denis where *Madame Louise* had been retreating for a few months, and then went to the Château de la Muette to introduce his future wife to the Count of Provence and the Count of Artois, and where she met the king's new and latest favorite, the Countess du Barry.

The official wedding was celebrated the next day, May 16, 1770, in the chapel of the Palace of Versailles, in the presence of 5,000 guests. There, Marie-Antoinette crossed the Hall of Mirrors with the king and her future husband to the chapel. The wedding was blessed by Charles Antoine de La Roche-Aymon, Archbishop of Reims. The dauphin, girded with the blue cordon of the order of the Holy Spirit, put the ring on his wife's finger and obtained the ritual sign of assent from the king. Then, the spouses and witnesses signed the parish registers. In the afternoon, the Parisians who had come in great numbers to attend the wedding were allowed to walk in the park of the castle where the water games had been activated. The fireworks planned for the evening were cancelled because of a violent storm. The dinner was organized in the brand new theater of the castle; the meal was accompanied by 24 musicians dressed in Turkish style. The couple ate very little. Shortly after midnight, they are accompanied to the bridal chamber. The archbishop blessed the bed, the dauphin received his bridal gown from the king and the dauphine from Marie-Adélaïde de Bourbon, duchess of Chartres, the highest-ranking married woman of the court. The audience attended the wedding, the king threw a few jokes and the bride and groom were left to their own devices. The marriage was not consummated that night, but seven years later.

The wedding celebrations continued the following days: the couple attended operas (*Persée* by Lully), plays (*Athalie*, *Tancrède* and *Sémiramis)*. They opened the ball organized in their honor on May 19. The festivities ended on May 30 when a fireworks display was planned from the Place Louis XV (where a few years later King Louis XVI and his wife were guillotined). Only the dauphine made the trip, the king having wanted to stay in Versailles and the dauphin having become tired of the festivities. As Marie-Antoinette and Mesdames arrived at the Cours la Reine, they were asked to turn back. It is only the next day that the dauphine will learn what happened: during the fireworks, a fire broke out in the rue Royale, creating a panic; many passers-by were crushed by cars and trampled by horses. The official death toll was 132 and hundreds were injured. The young couple was appalled. The dauphin immediately wrote to the lieutenant general of police Antoine de Sartine: "I learned of the misfortunes that happened on my occasion; I am deeply moved by them. They bring me at this moment what the King gives me every month for my small pleasures. I can only dispose of that. I send it to you: help the most unfortunate". The letter is accompanied by a sum of 6 000 livres.

Delicate subject of the consummation of the marriage

The consummation of the marriage of the dauphin, far from being a private affair, will quickly become an affair of state: through his descendants, it is not only his family but the whole monarchy that the future king must perpetuate. But this consummation will be effective only on August 18, 1777, that is to say more than 7 years after the marriage of the dauphin.

Why such a long wait? According to the writer Stefan Zweig, Louis-Auguste is the only one responsible. Victim of a malformation of the genitals, he would have tried every night to accomplish his conjugal duty, in vain. These daily failures are reflected in the life of the court, the dauphin who became king is unable to make important decisions and the queen compensates his misfortune in balls and parties. The author even suggests that the king is "incapable of manhood" and that it is therefore impossible for him "to behave like a king". Then, again according to the author, the couple's life returned to order the day Louis XVI finally deigned to accept to trust the surgery. Nevertheless, according to Simone Bertière, one of the biographers of Marie Antoinette, this physical infirmity was not the cause of the long abstinence of the couple, since the dauphin did not suffer from any such infirmity. Certainly, as early as July 1770 (only two months after the marriage), King Louis XV took advantage of a momentary absence of the dauphin to summon Germain Pichault de La Martinière, a renowned surgeon at the time. He asked him two very precise medical questions: "Does the young prince suffer from phimosis and is it necessary to circumcise him? Are his erections hindered by a brake that is too short or too strong that a simple lancet stroke could free? The surgeon is clear: "the dolphin has no natural defect that opposes the consummation of the marriage." The same surgeon will repeat it two years later by saying that "no physical obstacle opposes the consummation". The empress Marie-Thérèse of Austria took up the subject, refusing to believe that her daughter could be the cause of this failure, saying "I could not persuade myself that it is from her that this is lacking. In December 1774, having become king, Louis XVI was examined again, this time by Joseph-

Marie-François de Lassone, court physician; and in January 1776, Dr. Moreau, surgeon at the Hôtel-Dieu de Paris, was given the task of examining the sovereign again. The two doctors are formal: the operation is not necessary, the king has no malformation.

Doctors Lassone and Moreau nevertheless put forward several reasons for this marital delay, the first speaking of a "natural shyness" of the monarch and the second of a fragile body which nevertheless seemed to "take more consistency". Other authors, such as the biographer Bernard Vincent, denounce the customs of the court which, added to the shyness of the king and the fragility of his body, could only delay the supreme moment. Indeed, the spouses lived in separate apartments, and only the king had the right to visit his wife when it came to fulfilling the marital duty. Once he became king, Louis XVI lived in apartments even further away from his wife's than before, and the comings and goings to his wife were always under the gaze of curious courtiers, including through the salon de l'Œil-de-bœuf. The author adds that the prudish and prudish education of the two young spouses, at the time when they were educated each in their country, had not disposed them to abandon themselves overnight to the audacities of conjugal relations. For the adolescents, by being obliged to spend their first night together, were suddenly confronted with adult life without having been previously prepared for it.

And neither their education nor their barely pubescent bodies could help them overcome this stage. Not very confident [What?] and not very romantic, Louis XVI found refuge in one of his favorite activities: hunting.

Months and years passed without any real progress being perceived, as the Delphinian and then the royal couple began to get used to the situation. Marie-Antoinette saw this period as an opportunity to "enjoy a little of the time of youth," she explained to Mercy-Argenteau. A semblance of consummation occurs in July 1773 when the dauphin confides to her mother: "I believe the marriage consummated but not in the case of being fat". The dauphin rushed to the king to tell him the news. It seems in truth that the dolphin could only deflower his wife without going through with it. The wait is rewarded on August 18, 1777. On August 30, the princess wrote to her mother: "I am in the most essential happiness for all my life. It is already more than eight days since my marriage was consummated; the test was repeated, and again last night more completely than the first time [...]. I don't think I'm fat yet, but at least I have the hope of being able to be fat from one moment to the next. The fulfillment of the marital duty will bear fruit four times since the royal couple will have as many children, not counting a miscarriage in November 1780: Marie-Thérèse Charlotte (born in 1778), Louis-Joseph (born in 1781), Louis-Charles (born in 1785) and Marie-Sophie-Béatrice (born in 1786).

After these four births, the couple will no longer maintain conjugal relations. These failures and this new abstinence will give the king the image of a king subjected to the will of his wife. The long road to consumption has tarnished over time the image of the couple. And the writer Simone Bertière to affirm: "a voluntary chastity, respectful of the marital sacrament, could have been brought to his [Louis XVI's] credit after the libertinism of his grandfather. But the ridicule of the sterile years will stick to his image, while that of the queen will not recover from its imprudent race to the adulterated pleasures ".

Four years of life of the Delphinian couple

Between the marriage of the dauphin and his coronation, four years passed, during which Louis-Auguste was voluntarily kept away from power by the king, as the latter used to do with his own son. He therefore used his time for official ceremonies, hunting (with hounds or guns), the manufacture of keys and locks and the salons of the ladies. It is in these rooms that the dauphin meets his aunts and brothers, accompanied when the time comes by their wives. The games, entertainments and plays of the French repertoire occupy an important place. Each participant often acted, including the dauphine; the dauphin was not very inclined to do so.

The couple showed themselves willingly in public, especially by giving a few moments of comfort to the poor. The historian Pierre Lafue writes that "popular without having sought it, the two spouses shivered with joy listening to the acclamations going up to them, as soon as they appeared in public". Their first official visit to Paris and the Parisian people took place on June 8, 1773. During this day, the couple received a warm welcome and the large crowd did not stop cheering them. On the program of this long day, Louis-Auguste and his wife were received at Notre-Dame, went up to pray in front of the shrine of Saint Genevieve in the abbey of the same name before finishing with a walk in the Tuileries, open to all for the occasion. Mercy's ambassador summed up the day by saying that "this entry is of great consequence to fix public opinion". The couple took a liking to these triumphal welcomes and did not hesitate, in the following weeks, to go out to the Opera, to the Comédie-Française or to the Comédie-Italienne.

Death of Louis XV

Louis XV died in Versailles on May 10, 1774 at the age of 64, of smallpox.

The first symptoms of the disease appeared on April 27. On that day, the king was at Trianon and had planned to go hunting with his grandson, the Duke of Berry. Feeling feverish, the monarch followed the hunt in a carriage. A few hours later, his condition worsened and La Martinière ordered him to return to Versailles. Two days later, on

April 29, the doctors announced that the king had contracted smallpox, as had several members of his family before him (notably Hugues Capet and the Grand Dauphin). To avoid contagion, the dauphin and his two brothers were kept away from the royal bedroom. The king's face was covered with pustules on April 30. Not having any illusions about his health, he called in his confessor, Abbé Louis Maudoux, on the night of May 7. Extreme Unction was administered to him on the evening of May 9.

Around 4 pm the next day, the king breathed his last. The Duke of Bouillon, the great chamberlain of France, went down to the Bull's Eye and shouted the famous phrase: "The king is dead, long live the king! Hearing this from the other end of the castle, the brand-new monarch let out a loud shout and saw the courtiers who had come to greet him run up to him; among them was the Countess of Noailles, who would be the first to award him the title of Majesty. The king exclaims: "What a burden! And I have not been taught anything! It seems to me that the universe will fall on me! As for Queen Marie Antoinette, she would have sighed, "My God! protect us, we reign too young."

King of France and Navarre (1774-1791)

Accession to the throne and first decisions

Immediately after the death of Louis XV, the court took temporary refuge in the castle of Choisy-le-Roi, in order to avoid any risk of contagion and to leave the stinking atmosphere of the Versailles castle. It was on this occasion that the new king took one of his first decisions: to inoculate the entire royal family against smallpox. The aim of this operation was to administer a very low dose of contaminated substances into the human body, the subject then becoming immune for life. Nevertheless, the risk is real since a dose that is too large can cause the patient to contract the disease and thus die. On June 18, 1774, the king received five injections and his brothers only two each. The first symptoms of smallpox quickly appeared in the king: he suffered from armpit pain on June 22, was taken by fever and nausea on June 24; a few pimples appeared on June 27 and a slight suppuration occurred on June 30. But the fever fell on July 1er and the king was definitely out of danger. The operation was a success, both for him and for his two brothers, whose symptoms were almost imperceptible.

Among the first notable decisions of the new monarch, we can note three others: he had Madame du Barry locked up and took the name of *Louis XVI and* not that of *Louis-Auguste Ier* as logic would have it, in order to place himself in the line of his predecessors. Finally, he summoned all the ministers in place, provincial intendants and commanders of the armed forces nine days later. For the time being, he isolated himself in his office to work, correspond with the ministers, read reports and write letters to the European monarchs.

The economy of the Kingdom of France had been in recession since 1770. Thus, Louis XVI immediately began to reduce the expenses of the court: he reduced the "expenses of the mouth" and the expenses of the wardrobe, the department of Menus-Plaisirs, the hunting crews such as those of the fallow deer and the wild boar, the Small Stable (thus passing the contingent from 6 000 to 1 800 horses), and finally the number of musketeers and gendarmes assigned to the protection of the king. His brother, the Count of Artois, suspected him of avarice, calling him "a miserly King of France". The king made the poorest people benefit from his savings by distributing 100 000 pounds to the poorest Parisians. In addition, his first edict, dated May 30, exempted his subjects from the "gift of joyous advent", a tax levied upon the accession to the throne of a new king, which amounted to twenty-four million pounds. According to Metra, "Louis XVI seems to promise the nation the sweetest and most fortunate reign.

Ministers and new government

The new king decided to rule alone and did not consider delegating this task to a head of government. Nevertheless, he needed a man of confidence and experience to advise him in the important decisions he would have to make. This is the task of the man who is informally called the "Principal Minister of State". Louis XVI appointed seven of them successively during his reign:

- Jean Frédéric Phélypeaux de Maurepas (1774-1781);
- Charles Gravier de Vergennes (1781-1787): he exercised this power *de facto* because officially the king did not need a principal minister during this period;
- Étienne-Charles de Loménie de Brienne (1787-1788);
- Jacques Necker (1788-1789);
- Louis Auguste Le Tonnelier de Breteuil (1789) ;
- Jacques Necker again (1789-1790);

- and finally Armand Marc de Montmorin Saint-Hérem (1790-1791).

The function ends with the promulgation of the Constitution of 1791.

Marie-Antoinette suggested to the king to appoint to this function the duke of Choiseul, former minister of Louis XV who had fallen into disgrace in 1770. The king refused to appoint him as the main minister of state but agreed to reinstate him at court. He attended the meeting between the latter and the queen and said to her as an insult: "You have lost your hair, you are becoming bald, your head is not well furnished.

According to the historian Jean de Viguerie in his book entitled *Louis XVI, le roi bienfaisant (Louis XVI, the beneficent king)*, the two ministers who had the most influence with King Louis XVI during most of his reign were, first, the Count of Maurepas, and then, after the latter's death in 1781, the Count of Vergennes.

Failing to follow his wife's advice, the king chose the Count of Maurepas, on the advice of his aunts. This experienced man, disgraced by Louis XV in 1747, had for brother-in-law Louis Phélypeaux de Saint-Florentin and for cousin René Nicolas de Maupeou. On May 11, 1774, the day after the death of the monarch, Louis XVI wrote the following letter to Maurepas:

"Sir, in the just grief which overwhelms me and which I share with the whole Kingdom, I have nevertheless duties to fulfill. I am King: this word alone contains many obligations, but I am only twenty years old. I do not think I have acquired all the necessary knowledge. Moreover, I cannot see any minister, having been locked up with the King in his illness. I have always heard of your probity and the reputation that your deep knowledge of affairs has so rightly earned you. This is what leads me to ask you to kindly help me with your advice and insights. I will be obliged to you, Sir, to come as soon as you can to Choisy, where I will see you with the greatest pleasure.

Two days later, on May 13, 1774, the Count of Maurepas came to the King at Choisy to show his gratitude and to commit himself to his service. With a minister of state at his side, all that remained for the king to do was to convene the first council, during which he had to decide whether or not to keep the ministers already in place. This first council will not take place in Choisy but in the castle of La Muette, the court having to move again because Ladies suffer from symptoms of smallpox. The first council was held at the château de la Muette on May 20, 1774. The new king did not make any decisions, but simply got to know the ministers in place and gave them the line of conduct that should be theirs: "As I only want to take care of the glory of the kingdom and the happiness of my people, it is only by conforming to these principles that your work will have my approval".

The king proceeded to a gradual reshuffle of ministers. The change began on June 2, 1774 with the resignation of the Duc d'Aiguillon, Secretary of State for War and Foreign Affairs. Far from exiling him as was the custom, the king allocated him the sum of 500 000 francs. D'Aiguillon was replaced at the Foreign Office by the Count de Vergennes, a diplomat reputed to be competent and hard-working, "the wisest minister that France had met for a long time, and the most skilful who was in charge of affairs in Europe" according to the historian Albert Sorel.

Residing at the castle of Compiègne for the summer, the king, advised by Maurepas, undertook to replace some ministers in positions where great competence was needed. Thus, Pierre Étienne Bourgeois de Boynes was replaced by Turgot at the Navy, the former being dismissed for incompetence and obvious lightness, the latter appointed to this position primarily for his effective administration as intendant of the generality of Limoges. Turgot was nevertheless removed very quickly from the Navy to become Controller General of Finance, replacing Joseph Marie Terray; he was replaced in his previous position by Antoine de Sartine, former Lieutenant General of Police. The portfolio of Justice passed from Maupeou to Miromesnil. The duke of la Vrillière remained in the King's Household while the Secretary of State for War was entrusted to the count of Muy in replacement of Aiguillon. Muy died a year later and was replaced by the Count of Saint-Germain.

By August 24, 1774, when the new government was fully formed, the ministers in place were as follows:

- Main Minister of State: the Count of Maurepas;
- Comptroller General of Finance: Turgot ;
- Keeper of the Seals : Armand Thomas Hue de Miromesnil ;
- Secretary of State for War : Louis Nicolas Victor de Félix d'Ollières, count of Muy ;
- Secretary of State for the Navy : Antoine de Sartine ;
- Secretary of State for Foreign Affairs : Charles Gravier de Vergennes ;
- Secretary of State to the King's Household : Louis Phélypeaux de Saint-Florentin, duc de la Vrillière.

The announcement of the new government was widely welcomed and the people danced in droves in the streets.

Coronation ceremony

On June 11, 1775, in the cathedral of Reims, he was crowned according to the tradition dating back to Pepin the Short. The last coronation, that of Louis XV, took place on October 25, 1722; since then, the very principle of this ceremony was highly criticized by the Enlightenment movement: the *Encyclopedia* and the philosophers criticized the ritual, seeing in it only an exacerbation of God's power and a comedy intended to maintain the people in obedience. The general controller of finances, Turgot, reproached the monarch for this costly ceremony evaluated at 760 000 livres; a short time before, Nicolas de Condorcet had written to Turgot to ask him to do without "the most useless and ridiculous of all the expenses" of the monarchy. Turgot then thought of making a sort of light coronation, probably near the capital, in Saint-Denis or in Notre-Dame, to reduce the costs. However, pious and very attached to the work of his predecessors, even if he is determined to redress the economic situation in bad shape, the king does not back down on this and maintains the ceremony with as much pomp as planned.

The cathedral of Notre-Dame de Reims, emblematic place of the coronations of the kings of France, is transformed for the festivities, a real building being built inside, with balustrade, columns, chandeliers, fake marbles ... It is also the first time since Louis XIII that the king is married at the time of his coronation, which makes possible the coronation of his consort. But the last coronation of a queen, that of Marie de Medici on May 13, 1610 at the Basilica of Saint-Denis, had taken place as a dark omen, Henri IV having been assassinated the next day; moreover the queen, in the absolutist construction of power, had seen its political importance decrease. It was finally decided not to crown Marie-Antoinette. She attended the ceremony from the largest of the tribunes, with the important women of the Court.

The ceremony was presided over by the Archbishop of Rheims, Charles Antoine de La Roche-Aymon, the same one who had baptized and married the Dauphin. The ceremony lasted nearly six hours - a box for the spectators to rest was arranged behind the queen's tribune; all the steps took place, the king's rising, the entrance, the oath, the ritual of knighthood, the anointing, the presentation of the insignia, the coronation, the enthronement, the high mass, the homage of the peers, the low mass and the exit. According to tradition, the prelate pronounces the following formula while placing the crown of Charlemagne on the head of the sovereign: "May God crown you with glory and justice, and you will attain the eternal crown". In accordance with the ritual, the king then went to the city park to cure the scrofula of the 2,400 scrofula sufferers who had come for the occasion, addressing each of them with the ceremonial formula: "The king touches you, God heals you.

The royal couple will keep a very good memory of the ceremony and the following festivities. Marie-Antoinette wrote to her mother that "the coronation was perfect [...]. The ceremonies of the Church [were] interrupted at the moment of the coronation by the most touching acclamations. I could not stand it, my tears flowed in spite of myself, and I was thankful for it [...]. It is an astonishing thing and at the same time very happy to be so well received two months after the revolt, and in spite of the dearth of bread, which unfortunately continues.

First economic and financial measures of Turgot

As soon as the court returned to Versailles on September 1er, 1774, the king met daily with Turgot to prepare measures for the economic recovery of the country. The former Controller General of Finances, Abbé Terray, had suggested an official proclamation of bankruptcy of France, in front of the deficit of 22 million pounds existing at that time. Turgot refused to propose bankruptcy and suggested a simpler plan: to make savings. He said to the monarch: "If the economy has not preceded, no reform is possible". He encourages the king to continue to reduce the expenses of the court that he had already started.

Turgot was also a supporter of economic liberalism. On September 13, 1774, he had the king's council adopt a text decreeing the freedom of internal trade in grain and the free importation of foreign grain. The risk of sudden price increases in case of a bad harvest was nevertheless real. This is what happened in the spring of 1775: a rumor of imminent famine filled the country; prices soared and bakeries in Paris, Versailles and some provincial towns were looted; riots occurred but were quickly suppressed. This episode is known today as the "flour war". This popular revolt during the reign of Louis XVI is considered to be the first warning of the people about the economic difficulties of the country and the ineffective reforms of the royal power to solve them.

Reminder of parliaments

From the XIVe century until 1771, Parliaments had important powers in civil, political and judicial matters. Among the 15 parliaments existing at the end of the reign of Louis XV, the jurisdiction of the Parliament of Paris extended over 75% of the Kingdom of France. Every decision of a parliament had the force of law; moreover, every royal decree could only be enforced if it had first been registered (i.e. endorsed) by the competent parliament. Over the centuries, the power of the parliaments had continued to grow to the point of becoming an autonomous power that could compete with royal absolutism. A parliamentary pamphlet of 1732 went far in this direction by specifying that the king "can only contract with his people in the bosom of parliament, which, as old as the Crown and born with the State, is the representation of the entire monarchy. Tired of this increase in the powers of the parliaments, Louis XV and with him the chancellor Maupeou undertook in 1771 to purely and simply withdraw from the parliaments their powers, offices and privileges that they had granted themselves over the years. The new magistracy, organized in *Superior Councils*, was restricted to rendering justice free of charge and limited in its right of remonstrance.

Upon his accession, Louis XVI was to reverse this reform. On October 25, 1774, he summoned all the exiled magistrates to a meeting which he presided over on November 12 at the Palais de Justice in Paris. In front of the assembled parliamentarians, he addressed these words to them: "I call you back today to functions that you should never have left. Feel the price of my kindnesses and never forget them! [...] I want to bury in oblivion all that has happened, and I would see with the greatest displeasure internal divisions disturbing the good order and the tranquility of my parliament. Do not occupy yourselves but with the care to fulfill your functions and to answer my views for the happiness of my subjects which will always be my only object ". The same evening, fireworks were launched at the Pont Neuf and at the Palais de Justice to greet this return.

In the face of such a reversal, it is necessary to question the motives of Louis XVI in recalling and re-establishing the parliaments, for it may seem strange that the king should have chosen to weaken his power on his own. It may seem strange that the king himself chose to weaken his power. As the dauphin, he had repeatedly written about his opposition to the extended power of the parliaments, stating in particular that they "are not representatives of the nation", that they "have never been and can never be the organ of the Nation vis-à-vis the King, nor the sovereign organ vis-à-vis the Nation", and that their members are "mere depositaries of a part" of the royal authority. One of the reasons may lie in the popularity that the exiled parliaments had at the time. Indeed, despite their lack of representativeness of the people, they were supported by them. They publicly displayed their support for the new ideas and the need to respect natural rights: the king should therefore be a mere agent of the people and not an absolute sovereign. The king, in his youth and inexperience at the beginning of his reign, would therefore have acted in part to garner significant popular support; this, it should be remembered, is what happened in the streets of Paris immediately after the announcement of the recall of the parliaments. The other reason would reside in the attentive and followed advice of the Count of Maurepas, who believed that "without parliament, no monarchy!"

Attentive to his image with the people and confident in Maurepas' advice in the face of the complexity of the subject, Louis XVI thus reversed the privileges that Maupeou described at the time of his dismissal as "a trial that had been going on for three hundred years" and that he had helped the king win. This recall of the parliaments will make illusory the attempts of deep reforms that the king will consider to undertake in the following years, which will contribute to nourish the revolutionary climate that is already preparing. Madame Campan, Marie-Antoinette's chambermaid, would later write that "the century would not end without some great jolt shaking France and changing the course of its destiny.

Reforms and disgrace of Turgot

To ensure the future of the kingdom, Turgot will undertake a profusion of reforms aimed at unblocking the free political, economic and social functioning of society, and to bring the parliaments to heel.

As the historian Victor Duruy explained in 1854: "These were great novelties; Turgot planned other more formidable ones: abolition of the corvées which weighed on the poor; establishment on the nobility and the clergy of a territorial tax; but improvement of the fate of the parish priests and vicars, who had only the smallest portion of the revenues of the Church, and abolition of most of the monasteries; equal participation of the tax by creation of a cadastre; freedom of conscience and recall of the Protestants; redemption of the feudal annuities; a single code: one system of weights and measures for the whole kingdom; abolition of the jurands and masterships which enchained industry; thought as free as industry and commerce; finally, as Turgot was concerned with moral needs as well as material needs, a vast plan of public instruction to spread the Enlightenment everywhere."

Turgot wanted to abolish several practices that had been well established until then: abolition of jurands and guilds, abolition of certain customs forbidding, for example, apprentices to marry or excluding women from embroidery work. Abolition of serfdom and the royal corvée. In Turgot's plan, the corvée would be replaced by a single tax on all landowners, which would extend the payment of the tax to members of the clergy and nobility.

Turgot also embarked on a "revolutionary" project of setting up a pyramid of elected assemblies throughout the kingdom: municipalities of communes, of arrondissements, then of provinces, and a municipality of the kingdom. The purpose of these assemblies was to distribute direct taxes and to manage police, welfare and public works issues.

This vast project of reforms did not fail to meet a number of detractors, starting with the parliamentarians. Turgot could count on the support of the king, who did not fail on several occasions to practice the "bed of justice" to apply his decisions. Based on a remark made by a worker at his forge, he said in March 1776: "I can see that only Monsieur Turgot and I love the people. The support of the king is perceived as crucial for the minister, who will say to the sovereign: "Either you will support me, or I will perish". Opponents became more and more numerous and went beyond the circle of parliamentarians. A coalition was formed against Turgot and gathered, according to Condorcet, "the prêtraille, the routine parliaments and the scoundrels of financiers". Certainly, the people and the peasants welcomed with open arms the edicts abolishing the masterships, the jurandes and the royal corvée; troubles even broke out following the excess of enthusiasm. Nevertheless, the king began to receive letters of remonstrance from the parliaments, and to face criticism from the court. Louis XVI moderated and reminded the parliaments that the reforms undertaken were not intended to "confuse the conditions" (clergy, nobility, third estate).

The minister began to fall in the esteem of the king, who did not hesitate to say that "M. Turgot wants to be me, and I do not want him to be me. The disgrace becomes inevitable when Turgot takes part in the vote to remove the Count of Guines, ambassador in London, accused of practicing diplomacy to bring France into the war. De Guines was a friend of Marie-Antoinette and she asked the king to punish the two ministers who had asked for the resignation of the count, namely Malesherbes and Turgot. Disgusted by this request, Malesherbes resigned from the government in April 1776. The king distanced himself from Turgot and condemned all of his reforms: "One should not undertake dangerous undertakings if one cannot see the end of them," Louis XVI said. On May 12, 1776, a double news bursts: Turgot is dismissed, and the count of Guines is made duke. Turgot refused the pension that was offered to him, stating that he should "not give the example of being at the expense of the State".

Some historians refute the idea that the king had simply given in to his wife. The decision to dismiss Turgot (and especially to raise de Guines) would be more the "purchase" of the silence of the count, who would have been aware of many things about French diplomacy that could embarrass the king. Another reason for the dismissal would also reside in Turgot's refusal to finance France's intervention in the American War of Independence, as the poor state of the kingdom's finances did not allow it. In any case, this episode will be for historians the perfect illustration of the ascendancy of the queen over her husband, and will constitute the beginnings of the state of weakness of the king vis-à-vis his wife; the historian Simone Bertière writes that with each victory of the queen, "the prestige of the king is dented, his authority decreases as much as the credit of it increases. This is only appearance [but] authority, too, feeds on appearance." Turgot himself, in a letter written to Louis XVI on April 30, 1776, which the latter returned to him without even opening it, warned the king: "Never forget, Sire, that it was weakness that put the head of Charles Ier on a chopping block.

Turgot was replaced by Jean Étienne Bernard Clugny de Nuits, who hastened to reverse the main reforms of his predecessor, re-establishing in particular jurands and corvées, claiming that he could "knock down on one side what Mr. Turgot had knocked down on the other. But the minister quickly proved to be incompetent, and the king declared "I believe that we are still mistaken". Louis XVI did not have time to dismiss him, Clugny de Nuits died suddenly on October 18, 1776 at the age of 47.

Reforms and resignation of Necker

In October 1776, Louis XVI needed a minister of finance capable of undertaking reforms but not of destroying everything; he confided to Maurepas: "Don't talk to me about these masons who want to demolish the house first". He then thought of Jacques Necker, a banker from Switzerland, known for his art of handling money and his concern for economy. A triple revolution: he was a commoner banker, a foreigner (from Geneva) and moreover a Protestant. The king appointed him first of all "director of the Treasury" (the post of controller general of finance was given for the sake of form to Louis Gabriel Taboureau des Réaux) because Necker, a Protestant, could not access for this reason to the King's Council attached to the post of controller general. Nevertheless, the king appointed him "Director General of Finance" (the name was changed to give it more importance) on June 29, 1777, without admitting the minister to the Council.

Necker and Louis XVI reworked the most essential reforms of the kingdom, the minister's ambition being to replenish the coffers of the state without crushing the taxpayers or angering the rich and the owners. Necker understood that the ordinary expenses of the kingdom were financed by taxes; on the other hand, a way had to be found to finance exceptional expenses such as those generated by the American war of independence. Necker then created two lucrative systems with immediate returns: the loan and the lottery. Both systems were very successful with the people. However, these measures were only effective in the short term, as funds had to be borrowed to pay the lenders their life annuities and to pay the winners their prizes. In the long run, the debt would grow ever larger and a way had to be found again to establish a real structural reform.

For the time being, Necker proposed to the king to abolish the parliaments and intendants of the provinces, and to replace them by provincial assemblies recruited, on the king's proposal, from the clergy, the nobility and the third estate; the king undertook to favor the nobility of the sword and not the nobility of the robe. This project of institutional reform, already put on the table under Turgot, had as its objective that in the long run all assemblies should be directly elected. Although experimented in Bourges and Montauban, this reform was unanimously condemned by the intendants, the princes and the parliamentarians. The reform was therefore doomed to failure and would not see the light of day.

At the same time, Necker undertook a series of popular measures. First of all, he freed the last serfs of the royal domain by an ordinance of August 8, 1779. Refusing the indiscriminate abolition of personal servitude, he nevertheless abolished the "droit de suite" throughout the kingdom, and freed all the "main-mortables [serfs] of the king's domains", as well as the "hommes de corps", the "taillables" and the "taillables" [from which comes the expression "taillable et corvéable à merci"]. This ordinance had been favored by the intervention of Voltaire, who in 1778 had pleaded the cause of the serfs of the abbey of Saint-Claude du Mont-Jura. It also authorized the "engagists who believed themselves to be wronged" by this reform to hand over to the king the domains concerned in exchange for financial compensation. In order to encourage the imitation of his royal act of emancipation of the serfs in the royal domains, the ordinance specifies that "considering these emancipations much less as an alienation, than as a return to the natural right, we exempted these kinds of acts [of emancipation] from the formalities and taxes to which the ancient severity of the feudal maxims had subjected them. Nevertheless, the ordinance was hardly applied, and serfdom persisted locally until the Revolution, which abolished it with the privileges during the famous night of August 4, 1789. On August 8, 1779, an edict authorized married women, minors and religious to receive pensions without authorization (notably that of the husband in the case of married women). It also abolished the preparatory question, inflicted on suspects, and re-established the institution of the pawnshop.

In addition to this series of "republican" reforms and the unfortunate experimentation with provincial assemblies, the minister made a political error that would prove fatal. In February 1781, he sent the king an *account of the state of the finances* intended for publication. For the first time, he revealed to the general public the detailed use of public expenditure and revealed, in the interest of transparency, all the advantages enjoyed by the privileged members of the court. The latter disavowed the minister and denounced in return, with the support of financial experts, the deceptive balance sheet that the minister made of his action, hiding the debt of 46 million pounds left by the expenses of war, and underlining on the contrary a surplus of 10 million. "The war that had been so successful against Turgot began again under his successor," explains Victor Duruy.

Louis XVI and Necker could not hold out for long against the opposition of the privileged. The minister ended up losing the confidence of the king, the latter having said, commenting on the minister's record: "But it's Turgot and even worse! Necker asked the king to join the Council, but faced with the refusal of the sovereign, he handed him his resignation, which was accepted on May 21, 1781. According to the historian Jean-Louis Giraud-Soulavie, the letter of resignation was almost insulting since it was written on a simple "piece of paper three and a half inches long and two and a half inches wide".

Major changes during the department

- In 1775, the Duke of la Vrillière resigned from the Ministry of the King's Household and was replaced in this position by Malesherbes.

- Malesherbes left the government in April 1776, he was replaced by Antoine-Jean Amelot de Chaillou.

- Turgot was dismissed from his position as comptroller general of finance on May 12, 1776, and was replaced a few months later by Jacques Necker, after the two short-lived Clugny de Nuits and Taboureau des Réaux.

- On October 13, 1780, the Secretary of State for the Navy by de Sartine to the Marquis de Castries.

- Philippe Henri de Ségur was appointed Secretary of State for War on December 23, 1780.

- Necker resigned on May 19, 1781 and was replaced by Jean-François Joly de Fleury.

Vergennes Ministry

Maurepas died of gangrene on November 21, 1781. Louis XVI decided to dispense with his principal minister in order to live a period of "personal reign". As the most important minister after Maurepas was then Vergennes, the latter unofficially played a role of adviser to the king although he did not have the official recognition. This situation lasted until 1787 when Loménie de Brienne officially took over Maurepas' position.

Reform project and dismissal of Calonne

After the resignation of Necker, the post of Controller General of Finance was successively occupied by Joly de Fleury and d'Ormesson. On November 3, 1783, on the advice of Vergennes, Louis XVI appointed to this portfolio Charles Alexandre de Calonne, an intelligent man with a gift for communication, who had previously made remarkable proofs as intendant of the generality of Metz. Calonne was privately in debt, and said of his appointment: "The finances of France are in a deplorable state, I would never have taken charge without the poor state of mine. To solve this situation, the king gave him 100 000 pounds of installation expenses and 200 000 pounds of shares of the Compagnie des eaux de Paris.

At first, Calonne worked to restore the confidence of the French by trying to exploit the resources already existing in the kingdom, and to encourage industrial and commercial initiative. Then, in a second step, he undertook a careful but determined reform of the kingdom. In a speech given in November 1783 before the Chamber of Accounts, he evoked the idea of a "general improvement plan", "regenerating" resources rather than "pressurizing" them, in order to "find the real secret of reducing taxes in the proportional equality of their distribution, as well as in the simplification of their collection". The thinly veiled objective is thus to reform the entire tax system and, in so doing, to make up for the state's deficit.

On August 20, 1786, Calonne presented the king with his three-part plan of action:

- equality of all before the tax (abolition of the tax privileges of the nobility and the clergy, creation of a single tax based on the income from landed property (the "territorial subsidy");
- return to free movement of grain;
- creation of new assemblies elected by the landowners and which will have to associate the subjects of the King to the administration of the country.

This program, assures Calonne to the king, "will assure you more and more of the love of your people [and] will tranquilize you forever on the state of your finances".

Calonne's program allowed him to undertake major projects aimed at reviving industrial and commercial development; thus, he encouraged the renovation of the port of Le Havre, Dieppe, Dunkirk and La Rochelle and contributed to the repair of the sewerage system in the cities of Lyon and Bordeaux. He also created new factories. He was responsible for the signing of the Eden-Rayneval treaty on September 26, 1786, a trade treaty between France and Great Britain.

Calonne's fiscal and institutional reform made the king say: "But this is pure Necker that you are giving me! Faced with the reluctance of the parliaments, he convinced Louis XVI to convene an Assembly of Notables, bringing together members of the clergy, the nobility, the city bodies, and even delegates of the sovereign courts, not elected but appointed by the king. The objective of this assembly was to pass the main points of the reform by submitting them to the opinion (and therefore potentially to the approval) of its members. The assembly was held in Versailles on February 22, 1787. Calonne, in front of the 147 members gathered, tries to pass his reform; only, the admission that he makes of the public deficit of 12 million pounds moves the assistance. And Calonne loses all hope of persuasion when he justifies his project of reform by stating: "One cannot make a step in this vast kingdom without finding there different laws, contrary uses, privileges, exemptions, tax exemptions, rights and claims of all kinds! Faced with the outcry from an assembly of notables reluctant to approve a reform of which they would be the victims, Louis XVI did not feel the strength to counter the opponents and disapproved his minister.

The protests against Calonne's project are legion, the majority of the opponents considering that it goes too far, a handful thinking that it is insufficient and consequently bad. Calonne justifies himself on March 31 by crying out in a pamphlet: "Can one do good without offending some particular interests? Can one reform without complaints? Marie Antoinette openly asked for the dismissal of the minister; furious, Louis XVI summoned her in the presence of the Controller General of Finance, reprimanded her by asking her not to meddle in affairs "to which women have nothing to do" and made her leave holding her by both shoulders. Calonne is thanked on April 8, 1787, Easter day.

The fiasco of the assembly of notables is perceived by some historians as the real starting point of the Revolution. The biographer Bernard Vincent believes, for example, that "it is not illegitimate to start the French Revolution with the failure of Calonne and the rebellion of the notables in 1787 rather than with the storming of the Bastille or the meeting of the Estates General, as most textbooks do. After this fiasco, many indeed (but was Louis XVI one of them?) felt that an irreparable tear had just occurred in the fabric of the country and that a new history was already in motion."

Case of the Queen's Necklace

Designed in the early 1770s by jewelers Charles-Auguste Böhmer and Paul Bassenge, this 2,800-carat necklace was offered for sale to Louis XV as a gift to his ultimate mistress Madame du Barry, but the king died before buying it. On two occasions, in 1778 and 1784, Queen Marie-Antoinette refused the jewel although the king was ready to offer it to her.

One of the key characters in this affair is the Cardinal de Rohan, bishop of Strasbourg and former ambassador to Vienna. A debauchee, he is in love with Queen Marie-Antoinette. Only, he is not appreciated by her because he openly mocked her mother, Empress Maria Theresa of Austria. It is by wanting to return in the graces of the queen that he will be swindled in the affair of the necklace. On the night of August 11, 1784, he waits for a woman in the Versailles grove: he thinks it is the queen, but it is in fact a prostitute, Nicole Leguay, who comes to meet him, disguised and sent by Jeanne de Valois-Saint-Rémy, also called *Madame de La Motte*. The false queen confided to the cardinal: "You can hope that the past will be forgotten". Madame de La Motte soon afterwards told the cardinal that the queen wished to obtain the necklace without the king's knowledge, even if it meant paying for it in instalments: Rohan's role would therefore be to make the purchase in Marie-Antoinette's name. She then gave the cardinal an order form apparently signed by the queen but in fact by Louis Marc Antoine Rétaux de

Villette, who had forged the signature. Rohan saw nothing but fire and placed an order with the two jewelers for the sum of 1 600 000 livres payable in four installments, the first due date being July 31, 1785.

On July 12, 1785, the queen received a visit at the Trianon from Böhmer, one of the two jewelers. He gives her the bill of the first draft before leaving; not understanding this, the queen burns the bill. On August 1er , seeing nothing coming, Böhmer questions Madame Campan, Marie-Antoinette's chambermaid, who informs him that the bill is destroyed. Böhmer then exclaims, "Ah, Madame, this is not possible, the queen knows that she has money to give me!" The jeweler announces to Madame Campan that the order was placed by Rohan on the orders of the queen. Not believing it, the chambermaid advised him to speak directly to the queen. He was received on August 9, 1785 by Marie-Antoinette, who, hearing the story, fell to her death. She confessed that she had not ordered anything and had burned the bill. Furious, Böhmer retorted: "Madam, deign to admit that you have my necklace and make me give help or a bankruptcy will soon have revealed everything". The queen spoke to the king and, on the advice of Breteuil, then Minister of the King's Household, he decided to have Rohan arrested.

Cardinal Rohan was summoned by the king on August 15, 1785: he admitted his imprudence but denied being the instigator of the affair, a fault he blamed on Madame de La Motte. He was arrested the same day in liturgical vestments in the Hall of Mirrors, while on his way to the castle chapel to celebrate the Assumption Mass. He was imprisoned the same evening, but he took care to have his secretary destroy certain documents which, by their absence, concealed the truth about Rohan's true role. Rohan was accused of two things: swindling and lèse-majesté. Louis XVI gave him the choice of being judged by the Parliament of Paris for the crime or by himself for the crime. The second option had the advantage of judging the case discreetly without exposing everything in broad daylight, but Rohan nevertheless chose to be tried by the Parliament.

The trial of Cardinal Rohan took place in May 1786. The accused was supported by the influential members of the House of Rohan and by the bishops and the Holy See. Public opinion was also in favor of his acquittal since the story of the forged signature did not convince the people and the queen, having burned the bill, could not prove his innocence. Rohan was acquitted by a decision of May 31, 1786 by 26 votes to 22. Convinced of the guilt of the clergyman, Louis XVI exiled him to the Abbey of La Chaise-Dieu.

The king and queen, and more broadly the monarchical system itself, are the victims of this affair since they are singled out by the people. Marie-Antoinette was devastated, confiding to her friend Madame de Polignac: "The judgment that has just been pronounced is a terrible insult [but] I will triumph over the wicked by tripling the good that I have always tried to do. The holding of a public trial resulted in an unpacking by the press and sympathy for Cardinal Rohan. As a spectator of the triumphal exit of the cardinal from the Bastille to his place of exile, Goethe remarked: "By this reckless, unheard-of enterprise, I saw the royal majesty undermined and soon destroyed.

Recovery of the French Navy and visit to the Cherbourg shipyard

In the aftermath of the American War of Independence, Louis XVI undertook to improve the French navy in order to give the kingdom the means to defend itself in case of a new war. In 1779, he chose to establish a naval base in Cherbourg and decided to build a 4 kilometer long dike between Pelee Island and Querqueville Point. On the colonial question, Louis XVI took two contradictory measures the same year in 1784: the offer of bonuses to the owners of slave ships and in December "the ordinances of the Leeward Islands", promulgating an improvement of the fate of slaves in Saint-Domingue.

On June 20, 1786, Louis XVI began a trip to Cherbourg to see the progress of the work. Apart from the coronation in Reims and the flight to Varennes, this was the only provincial trip of the sovereign during his reign. Accompanied by Castries and Segur, he was warmly welcomed by the crowd and distributed pensions and tax exemptions to the people. The visit to the construction site began as soon as the king arrived on June 23: he sailed around the harbor in a canoe, listened to the explanations of the director of the works, the Marquis de Caux, on the Île Pelée, inspected the Gallet pit and presided over a grand dinner that evening. The next day, June 24, he attended several maritime maneuvers aboard the *Patriote*; a witness recounts that the king made "questions and observations whose sagacity astonished the sailors who had the honor of approaching". He wrote to Marie-Antoinette: "I have never tasted the happiness of being king better than on the day of my coronation and since I have been in Cherbourg. The maritime historian Etienne Taillemite wondered in 2002: "Acclaimed at each of his appearances by a crowd as immense as it was enthusiastic, he was able to measure the royalist fervor that was then the people's, since [during this trip] not a single false note could be noticed. How could he not understand that he possessed a major asset capable of countering all the intrigues of the Versailles and Parisian microcosm? The same historian adds: "[One could dream that the king] would know how to carry out the renovation of the kingdom as he had known how to carry out the renovation of his navy".

Major Departmental Changes

- After the death of Vergennes on February 13, 1787, Louis XVI appointed the Count of Montmorin as Secretary of Foreign Affairs.

- Dismissed on April 9, 1787, the Keeper of the Seals Miromesnil was replaced in this position by Lamoignon.

Brienne Ministry (1787-1788)

Vergennes died on February 13, 1787; it was not until May 3 of the same year that Louis XVI resumed the tradition of appointing a Principal Minister of State, which he did by calling to this post Étienne-Charles de Loménie de Brienne, who also became head of the Royal Council of Finance (the post of Comptroller General of Finance having been given for form's sake to Pierre-Charles Laurent de Villedeuil, after a short stint in the hands of Michel Bouvard de Fourqueux).

Arm wrestling between the king and the parliament

Archbishop of Toulouse, known to be an atheist and reputed to have dissolute morals, Brienne had presided over the assembly of notables and in this capacity attacked Calonne and his reform project. Now in charge of affairs, he was urged by the king to continue the efforts of his mediate predecessor; he therefore took up the essence of the project he himself had condemned. Faced with such resistance, the king and his minister decided to dissolve the assembly on May 25, 1787. The laws then went through the ordinary process of being registered by the parliament, which again was no small matter.

Parliament nevertheless began to validate the principle of free movement of grain and the establishment of provincial and municipal assemblies. Nevertheless, on July

2, 1787, the parliamentarians refused to register the edict creating the territorial subsidy necessary to reduce the deficit. On July 16, the parliamentarians persisted in their refusal, invoking, like La Fayette before them, that "only the Nation gathered in its states general can consent to a perpetual tax."

Tired of the resistance of the parliament, Louis XVI convened it on August 6, 1787 in a bed of justice: the mere reading of the edicts by the king gave them the force of law. The next day, however, the parliament pronounced the bed of justice null and void, a first in the life of the monarchy. A week later, the magistrate Duval d'Eprémesnil declared that it was time to "débourbonailler" and to give back to the parliament its powers. Calonne, against whom an investigation was opened for "depredations", took refuge in England, which made him the first emigrant of the Revolution.

On August 14, 1787, on the initiative of Brienne, the king exiled the parliament to Troyes. Each parliamentarian received a letter of seal and executed it. The reception in Troyes was triumphant and the provincial parliaments joined forces, as well as the Chamber of Accounts and the Court of Aids. The king capitulated on August 19 by officially renouncing the edict of territorial subsidy and promised the convocation of the Estates General for 1792. The parliament returned to Paris to the applause of the crowd. The crowd points at Calonne, Brienne and Marie-Antoinette, whose effigies are burned. The agitation then reaches the province.

The territorial subsidy having been abandoned, Brienne saw only one way to replenish the kingdom's coffers: recourse to loans. Convinced, Louis XVI convened a "royal session" of parliament on November 19, 1787, to accept a loan of 420 million livres over 5 years. During this session, the members of parliament protested against this unusual form of "royal session" and demanded the convocation of the Estates General for 1789. The king accepted the idea without specifying a date and asked for the immediate vote of the loan, declaring: "I order that my edict be registered". The Duke of Orleans said: "It's illegal!" and the king replied: "Yes, it's legal. It is legal because I want it! Following this session of November 19, the five-year loan was launched and the rebels were punished: the councilors Fréteau and Sabatier were arrested and the duke of Orleans was exiled to his land of Villers-Cotterêts.

Edict of Versailles and abolition of the preliminary question

During the winter of 1787-1788, the parliament entered into a sort of "truce" as it registered several royal texts without difficulty, among which :

- on the one hand, the Edict of Tolerance of Versailles (dated November 7, 1787 and registered on January 29, 1788) giving Protestants a civil status and the right to worship in private;
- on the other hand, the royal decree of 1er May 1788 abolishing the preliminary question.

At the same time, Malesherbes was considering the possible emancipation of the Jews of France.

Towards the convening of the Estates General

In the early months of 1788, Louis XVI and his ministers Brienne and Lamoignon considered restricting the powers of parliament to matters of justice and reserving the verification and registration of royal acts, edicts and ordinances for a "plenary court" whose members would be appointed by the king. The parliamentarians, protesting against this idea, anticipated this institutional reform and published a *Declaration of the Fundamental Laws of the Kingdom* on May 3, 1788, in which they recalled that they alone were the guardians of these laws and that the creation of new taxes was the responsibility of the Estates General. Furious, the king reacted two days later by overturning this declaration and requesting the arrest of the two main instigators of the revolt, d'Eprémesnil and Monsabert who, after taking refuge in the parliament, finally surrendered before being imprisoned.

On May 8, 1788, Louis XVI convened a new lit de justice and registered his reform. Lamoignon announced the transfer of an entire section of the parliament's powers to the *grand bailliage* (47 courts of appeal), and moreover, control over the laws of the kingdom would only be carried out by the "Plenary Court", which was still being planned. But as soon as the edict of May 8 was promulgated, most of the parliaments began to resist, such as those of Nancy, Toulouse, Pau, Rennes, Dijon, Besançon and Grenoble. On the date set for the first session of the Plenary Court, the few peers and dukes who had made the trip to Versailles resigned themselves to wandering the corridors of the château for lack of participants; one witness reported that the reform was "dead before it was born.

On July 21, 1788, an assembly of the three orders of the Dauphiné met without authorization at the Château de Vizille, not far from Grenoble: the assembly included 176 members of the third estate, 165 members of the nobility and 50 members of the clergy. Led by Antoine Barnave and Jean-Joseph Mounier, the assembly decreed the re-establishment of the States of Dauphiné and demanded the rapid holding of the States General of the kingdom, with the doubling of the number of deputies of the Third Estate and the introduction of the vote by head.

Faced with such a large movement, the king and Brienne cancelled the creation of the Plenary Court and, on August 8, 1788, announced the convocation of the Estates General for May 1er 1789. During the summer of 1788, the state stopped making payments for six weeks, and on August 16, the state of bankruptcy was proclaimed. Brienne resigned on August 24, 1788 (he was created a cardinal the following December 15).

Ministry Necker (1788-1789)

Faced with the bankruptcy of the State, Louis XVI called upon Necker once again, on August 25, 1788. Necker took over the finance portfolio with the title of Director General of Finance and, for the first time, was also appointed Principal Minister of State, succeeding Brienne. The Garde des Sceaux Lamoignon left his place to Barentin.

Economic disaster

In addition to the state of insolvency and bankruptcy of the kingdom, the climate in 1788 was calamitous: a rotten summer ravaged the harvests, and the freezing winter brought temperatures of -20°C to a standstill, paralyzing the mills, freezing the rivers and breaking up the roads. Wheat was in short supply and the people were hungry.

The beginning of 1789 saw several riots in France, some of which were violently repressed; the price of bread and the economic context were the main causes. In March, the cities of Rennes, Nantes and Cambrai were the scene of violent demonstrations; in Manosque, the bishop was stoned to death because he was accused of colluding with the grain grabbers; houses were looted in Marseille. Little by little, the riots spread to Provence, Franche-Comté, the Alps and Brittany. From April 26 to 28, the "Boulevard Saint-Antoine riot" was severely repressed by the men of the Swiss general Baron de Besenval who, having received the orders reluctantly given by the king, had some 300 demonstrators killed. It was in this climate of violence that the Estates General were to open.

Preparation of the General Assembly

The parliamentarians, who had enjoyed great popularity up to that point, were soon to be discredited by public opinion by recklessly revealing their conservatism. On September 21, 1788, the Parliament of Paris and other parliaments with it demanded that the Estates General be convened in three separate chambers, voting by order, as had been the case during the previous Estates General of 1614, thus preventing any major reform.

Louis XVI and Necker, on the other hand, were in favor of a more modern form of voting by encouraging the doubling of the Third Estate and the vote by head (thus changing to a number of votes per deputy, and not by order, which would have the effect of opposing the Third Estate, counting for one vote, to the clergy and the nobility, counting for two). They convened the Assembly of Notables on October 5, 1788 to deal with these two points; within this assembly two camps were distinguished: that of the "patriots" in favor of the doubling of the third party and the vote by head, and that of the "aristocrats", supporter of the forms of 1614. The assembly of notables met in Versailles from November 5. Except for a few deputies such as the count of Provence, La Rochefoucauld and La Fayette, the assembly pronounced itself by a very large majority in favor of the forms of 1614, the only ones to be according to it "constitutional". The king maintained his position and turned again to the parliaments, the opinion of the assembly of notables being only consultative.

On December 5, 1788, the Parliament of Paris accepted the doubling of the Third, but did not pronounce itself on the question of the vote by order or by head. Louis XVI became angry and declared to the members of parliament: "it is with the assembly of the Nation that I will conciliate the appropriate dispositions to consolidate, for ever, the public order and the prosperity of the State". On December 12, the count of Artois gives to his brother the king a memorandum condemning the vote by head. On December 27, after Louis XVI had dissolved the assembly of notables, the King's Council met and officially accepted the doubling of the Tiers; the system of voting, by order or by head, was not yet settled. The royal decree also specified that the election of deputies would be by bailiwick and by proportional representation; moreover, it was decided that simple priests, in practice close to the ideas of the Third Estate, could represent the clergy.

On January 24, 1789, the royal letters were published giving details about the election of deputies. The king declared: "We need the help of our faithful subjects to help us overcome all the difficulties we are facing". Any French male of at least 25 years of age and registered in the roll of contributions can take part in the vote. For the nobility and the clergy, the constituency was the bailliage and the seneschaussée (depending on the region); for the Third Estate, suffrage was carried out in two stages in the countryside (parish assemblies and then chief town assemblies) and in three stages in the larger towns (corporation assemblies, town assemblies and bailliage or seneschaussée assemblies).

Each chief town assembly had the task of gathering the grievances in a book, a copy of which was sent to Versailles. Most of the claims expressed in the book were moderate and did not question the power in place or the existence of the monarchy.

Intellectuals, including Marat, Camille Desmoulins, Abbé Grégoire and Mirabeau, wrote numerous pamphlets and articles. Among these publications, the one by Sieyès entitled *Qu'est-ce que le Tiers-État?* met with great success; the following excerpt has remained famous:

On May 2, 1789, all the deputies were received at Versailles. Out of a total of 1,165, 1,139 were present (the deputies from Paris had not yet been designated): 291 from the clergy (including 208 simple priests), 270 from the nobility and 578 from the Third Estate. The historian Jean-Christian Petitfils notes that "the elected members of the first two orders were entitled to the opening of the two doors, while those of the third state had to be satisfied with only one!

On May 4, the day before the opening of the Estates General, a solemn mass was celebrated in the church of Saint-Louis in the presence of the royal family (except for the dauphin, who was too ill to leave his room). The homily of the celebrant, the bishop of Nancy Monseigneur de La Fare (also a deputy of the clergy), lasted more than an hour. The prelate began with a clumsy pronouncement: "Sire, receive the tributes of the clergy, the respects of the nobility and the very humble supplications of the Third Estate". Then he turns to Marie-Antoinette and stigmatizes those who squander the state's money; then addressing the king again, he declares: "Sire, the people have given unequivocal proof of their patience. They are a martyred people to whom life seems to have been left only to make them suffer longer. Back at the castle, the queen collapsed and the king was indignant. The next day, May 5, 1789, the Estates General will be opened and, by the same token, the French Revolution.

Foreign policy

Louis XVI was supported in foreign policy by Charles Gravier de Vergennes from 1774 to his death on February 13, 1787.

Role in the American War of Independence

Reasons for the king's involvement

The king's determination in gaining independence for the United States intrigues his biographers.

Most of them saw Louis XVI's involvement as revenge for the failures suffered by the kingdom of France during the Seven Years' War, at the end of which the country had lost its North American possessions. Thus, the revolt of the Thirteen Colonies was an unhoped-for opportunity to defeat the enemy.

However, some historians and biographers such as Bernard Vincent put forward another cause: that of Louis XVI's adherence to new ideas and his potential membership in Freemasonry: "Whether in the early days of his reign he was a member of the Order or a simple sympathizer or occasional visitor, the measured but undoubtedly real attention that Louis XVI devoted to the debate of Masonic ideas could only strengthen his determination to fly to the aid of the *insurgents* in America when the time came. The action of the Freemasons is indeed not insignificant in the access of the United States to independence, as testifies in particular the support brought by the French lodge of Nine Sisters.

The king may also have been influenced by Victor-François, duc de Broglie who, in a memorandum dated early 1776, drew the attention of the sovereign to the reality of the conflict between Great Britain and the American colonies. It is a question here, he says, of "an absolute revolution, [...] of a continent which is going to separate from the other" and that "a new order [...] is going to be born." He adds that it is in the interest of France "to take advantage of the distress of England to complete the burden.

Actions in the course of the conflict

France's intervention with the American colonists was initially clandestine. In September 1775, Julien Alexandre Achard de Bonvouloir went there to study the possibilities of discreet assistance to the insurgents. These negotiations lead, in 1776, to the secret sale of arms and ammunition and to the granting of subsidies for two million pounds. Beaumarchais received authorization from the king and Vergennes to sell gunpowder and ammunition for nearly one million livres tournois under the cover of the Portuguese company *Rodrigue Hortalez et Compagnie*. The first convoy, capable of arming 25,000 men, reached Portsmouth in 1777 and played a crucial role in the American victory at Saratoga.

Shortly after the victory at Saratoga, the American Congress sent two emissaries to Paris to negotiate greater French aid: Silas Deane and Benjamin Franklin. Joined by Arthur Lee, they succeeded in signing two treaties with Louis XVI and Vergennes, committing both countries: the first, a treaty of "friendship and commerce," in which France recognized American independence and organized mutual protection of maritime exchanges; the second, a treaty of alliance signed at Versailles on February 6, 1778, stipulating that France and the United States would make common cause in the event of a conflict between France and Britain. This treaty was the only alliance text signed by the United States until the North Atlantic Treaty of April 4, 1949. One month after the signing of the treaty, Conrad Alexandre Gérard was appointed by the king as minister plenipotentiary to the American government; Benjamin Franklin became his country's ambassador to the French court.

According to Vergennes, Minister of Foreign Affairs, the decision to ally with the Americans was taken by Louis XVI alone, in a sovereign manner. He testifies to this in a letter dated January 8, 1778 to the Count of Montmorin, then ambassador to Spain: "The supreme decision was taken by the king. It is not the influence of his ministers that decided him: the evidence of the facts, the moral certainty of the danger and his conviction alone led him. I could say with truth that His Majesty gave us all courage". This decision turns out to be risky in more than one way for the king: risk of defeat, risk of bankruptcy, and also risk to see arriving in France in the event of victory the revolutionary ideas little compatible with the monarchy.

Hostilities between the French and British forces began during the battle of June 17, 1778: the frigate *HMS Arethusa* was sent by the *Royal Navy* off Plouescat to attack the French frigate *Belle Poule*. Despite numerous victims, the kingdom of France emerged victorious. Louis XVI used this British aggression to declare war on his cousin George III of the United Kingdom on the following July 10; he declared: "the insults to the French flag have forced me to put an end to the moderation I had proposed and do not allow me to suspend the effects of my resentment any longer. The French ships were then ordered to fight the English fleet. The first confrontation between the two fleets took place on July 27, 1778: it was the Battle of Ushant, which saw France victorious and Louis XVI adored by his people.

While Spain and the Netherlands decided to join the conflict on the side of France, Louis XVI undertook to engage his naval forces in the American war. At the same time as this new stage in the conflict, Louis XVI signed a declaration of armed neutrality on March 9, 1780, uniting France, Spain, Russia, Denmark, Austria, Prussia, Portugal and the Two Sicilies against Great Britain and its attack on the freedom of the seas.

The king appointed Count Charles Henri d'Estaing to command the fleet sent to help the American *insurgents*. At the head of 12 ships of the line and 5 frigates, he carried with him more than 10 000 sailors and a thousand soldiers. The Fleet of the Levant left Toulon on April 13, 1778 to arrive off Newport (Rhode Island) on July 29. Apart from a victory at Grenada, the command of the

Count d'Estaing was characterized by a series of bitter failures for France, illustrated in particular by the Siege of Savannah during which he lost 5,000 men.

Urged on by his Spanish ally, Louis XVI had about 4,000 men assembled near Bayeux, with the goal of landing on the Isle of Wight and then in England via Southampton. The king was reluctant to take part in the operation and thought, if not to invade England, at least to keep the English ships in the Channel, thus weakening their participation in the war across the Atlantic. But the Franco-Spanish fleet could not dislodge the English ships protecting the island and changed course; dysentery and typhus struck the men, and neither the commander of this army, Louis Guillouet d'Orvilliers, nor his successor, Louis Charles du Chaffault de Besné, succeeded in a direct confrontation with the English fleet. The project had to be abandoned.

On the advice of Vergennes, the Count of Estaing, and La Fayette, Louis XVI decided to concentrate the forces of the French fleet on America. Thus, Jean-Baptiste-Donatien de Vimeur de Rochambeau was placed at the head of an expeditionary force on March 1er of 5,000 men. He left Brest on May 2, 1780 and arrived in Newport on July 10. On January 31, 1781, Lafayette asked Vergennes and Louis XVI to reinforce French naval power and to increase financial aid to the American forces. ^{er}The king was convinced of the merits of these requests; he granted the United States a gift of 10 million pounds and a loan of 16 million, and on June 1, 1781, he sent the money and two cargoes of arms and equipment from Brest. A few weeks earlier, Admiral de Grasse had left Brest for Martinique to bring reinforcements in ships and men. The combined tactics of the Franco-American infantry and Admiral de Grasse's fleet made it possible to inflict heavy losses on Admiral Thomas Graves' squadron and thus on the British fleet: the Battle of Chesapeake Bay and the Battle of Yorktown resulted in the defeat of England. On October 19, 1781, General Charles Cornwallis signed the surrender of Yorktown.

The participation of the kingdom of France in the victory of the United States is celebrated throughout the American territory and Louis XVI is not forgotten: for years, the king is the subject of enthusiastic demonstrations organized by the American people. The Treaty of Paris, signed on September 3, 1783 between the representatives of the thirteen American colonies and British representatives, ended the War of Independence. On the same day, the Treaty of Versailles was signed between France, Spain, Great Britain and the Netherlands.Under the terms of this act, Senegal and the island of Tobago belonged to France.

Impacts of American independence on France

American independence is undoubtedly a victory for France and its king, who largely contributed to the victory of the insurgents. Nevertheless, the birth of this new country made it possible to introduce on French soil an example of democracy that did not wait to implement new ideas: Declaration of Independence, emancipation of blacks in the northern states, women's right to vote in New Jersey, separation of powers, absence of official religion and recognition of freedom of the press in particular. Paradoxically, these revolutionary ideas that Louis XVI had helped to bring about by promoting American independence would be the cause of his downfall. For, as the journalist Jacques Mallet du Pan would later say, this "American inoculation has infused [the republican spirit] into all reasoning classes.

Relations with Austria

In 1777, Marie-Antoinette's brother Joseph II went to France to convince the king to give his support so that the Austrian Empire could annex Bavaria and begin the dismemberment of Turkey. Louis XVI rejected this request and France, contrary to the first partition of Poland in 1772, did not take part in the conflict.

The Treaty of Teschen was signed on May 13, 1779 between Austria and Prussia and put an end to the War of the Bavarian Succession. France and Russia are guarantors of its respect.

Louis XVI firmly opposed the claims of Joseph II of the Holy Roman Empire to reopen the mouths of the Scheldt to trade in the Austrian Netherlands, despite the pressure that Marie-Antoinette put on her husband.

Relations with Switzerland

In 1782, a coalition of rebels took power in Switzerland. France, contrary to what it had done for the United States, contributed to the repression of this rebellion and sent reinforcements to re-establish the power in place. Vergennes justified this intervention by affirming that it was necessary to avoid that Geneva becomes "a school of sedition".

Relations with Holland

In July 1784 the revolt of the "patriots" broke out in Holland, demanding that *Stathouder* William V of Orange-Nassau dismiss the conservative Duke of Brunswick. France took the side of the "patriots" and still supported them when William V was deposed in September 1786. However, the latter was reinstated in his functions in 1787: the "patriots" were crushed and France suffered a bitter diplomatic failure.

Other diplomatic relations

He continued the traditional French policy of supporting Catholic missions in the Near East. Faced with the vacuum created by the banning of the Society of Jesus (the Jesuits) in 1773, he chose the Lazarists to replace them in the missions in Ottoman territory. Pope Pius VI accepted this change, symbolized by the taking over of the center of the Catholic missions in the East, St. Benedict's High School in Constantinople, by the Congregation of the Mission of St. Vincent de Paul on July 19, 1783.

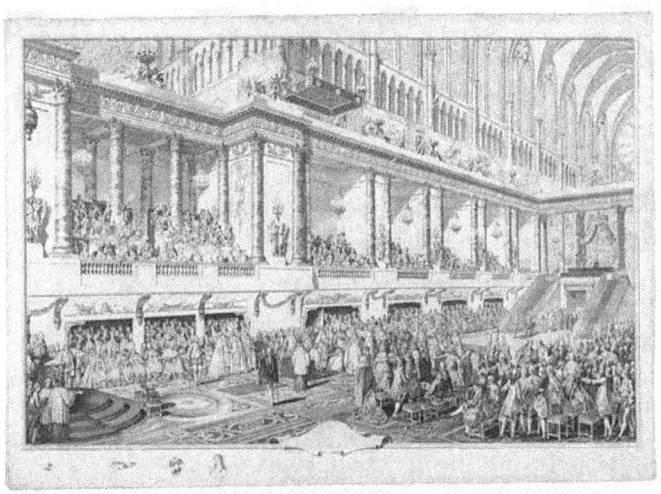

Beginnings of the Revolution

Opening (May 5, 1789)

The Estates General opened on May 5, 1789 at about 1:00 pm with a solemn opening session in the Menus-Plaisirs room in Versailles. The event took place in difficult conditions for the king, because for more than a year, the little dauphin Louis Joseph Xavier François was ill, which did not favor the contact between the king and the third estate. The dauphin died on June 4, which deeply affected the royal family.

During the session, the king is enthroned at the back of the room; on his left sit the members of the nobility, on his right those of the clergy and, opposite, those of the third estate. For the occasion, Louis XVI wore the fleurdelysed coat of the Order of the Holy Spirit and a feathered hat, in which the Regent, in particular, was seen.

The ceremony began with a brief speech by the king in which he declared, among other things: "Gentlemen, the day that my heart has been waiting for for a long time has finally arrived, and I see myself surrounded by the representatives of the Nation to which I take pride in commanding. He then briefly explains the course of recovery of the finances but warns against any attempt at reform: "A general concern, an exaggerated desire for innovations have seized the minds, and would end up completely misleading the opinions if one did not hasten to fix them by a meeting of wise and enlightened opinions.

Under a thunder of applause, the king leaves the word to the Garde des Sceaux Barentin. The latter praises the sovereign, recalling that the French have thanks to him a free press, that they made their own the idea of equality, and that they are ready to fraternize; but in his declaration are treated neither the mode of vote of the three orders, nor the state of the finances of the kingdom.

Then comes the turn of Necker. During a speech of more than 3 hours (pronounced by an assistant after a few minutes), he loses himself in vain flatteries and reminds the existence of the deficit of 56 million pounds. With no overall plan and no new announcements, he disappointed his audience. He finally asserted his position on the voting system, declaring himself in favour of a vote by order.

The king finally adjourned the session. For many deputies, this day was boring and disappointing.

Debates on the voting method

On May 6, the deputies of the Third Estate meet in the great hall and take, as in England, the name of *communes*. They propose to the clergy and to the nobility, who immediately vote separately, to proceed together to the verification of the powers of the deputies, but they meet a refusal of the two orders.

On May 11, the deputies of the nobility decided, by 141 votes against 47, to constitute themselves in a separate chamber and to verify in this way the powers of its members. The decision was more nuanced among the clergy, where, by a margin of a few votes, it was also decided to sit separately (133 for and 114 against). Conciliators were appointed to mitigate the differences but they admitted their failure on May 23.

On May 24, Louis XVI personally requested that conciliation efforts continue. However, he did not dialogue directly with the members of the third party, since Barentin played the role of intermediary.

On June 4, the dauphin Louis-Joseph of France died at the age of 7. The royal couple was deeply affected by the death of the pretender to the throne, but this event occurred in general indifference. His little brother Louis de France, the future Louis XVII, was now the dauphin at the age of 4.

Proclamation of the National Assembly (June 17, 1789)

On June 17, the deputies of the Third Estate took note of the refusal of the nobility to join them. Strengthened by the growing support of the clergy (several members joined them daily), and believing they represented "at least ninety-six hundredths of the nation", they decided, through the intermediary of the representative they had elected, the mathematician and astronomer Jean Sylvain Bailly, to proclaim themselves a *national assembly* and to declare purely and simply illegal the creation of any new tax without their agreement. The constitution of this assembly, proposed by Sieyès, is voted by 491 votes against 89.

On June 19, the clergy decided to join the Third Estate. The same day, the king discusses with Necker and Barentin. Necker proposes a plan of reforms close to the claims of the Third State: vote by head and equality of all in front of the tax in particular. Barentin, for his part, asked the king not to give in to the demands and declared: "Not to crack down is to degrade the dignity of the throne". The king did not decide anything for the moment and proposed to hold a "royal session" on June 23 where he would express his wishes.

Oath of the Jeu de paume

On June 20, the deputies of the Third Estate discovered that the Salle des Menus-Plaisirs was closed and barred by French guards. Officially, the assembly of June 23 was being prepared; in reality, Louis XVI had decided to close the room because, not only crushed by the mourning of the death of the dauphin, but also influenced by the queen, Barentin and other ministers, he felt betrayed by a Third Estate that had escaped his control and did not wish to meet until the assembly of June 23.

The deputies of the Tiers then decide, on the proposal of the famous doctor Guillotin, to find another room to meet. It is then that they enter in the room of the Game of palm, located at two steps. It is in this room that the assembly, at the initiative of Jean-Joseph Mounier, declares itself "called to fix the constitution of the kingdom" then, unanimously except one vote, it lends the oath to "never separate" as long as a new constitution will not be given to the kingdom of France. It finally declares that "wherever its members are gathered, there is the National Assembly!"

On June 21, Louis held a Council of State at the end of which the plan proposed by Necker on June 19 was rejected, despite the support of ministers Montmorin, Saint-Priest and La Luzerne.

Royal Session

The royal session decided by the king opened in the large room of the hotel of Menus-Plaisirs, in the absence of Jacques Necker but in the presence of a troop largely deployed for the occasion. Louis XVI gave a brief speech in which he announced his decisions. Noting the lack of results of the Estates General, he called the deputies to order: "I owe it to the common good of my kingdom, I owe it to myself to stop your disastrous divisions. He declared that he was in favor of equality of taxation, individual liberty, freedom of the press, the disappearance of serfdom, and the abolition of the letters of seal, which he would decide on June 26; on the other hand, he declared null and void the proclamation of the National Assembly of June 17, and maintained his intention to have the three orders vote separately. He finally recalls that he incarnates the only legitimate authority of the kingdom: "If, by a fate far from my thought, you would abandon me in such a beautiful company, only I would make the good of my people, only would consider me as their true representative". The meeting is closed and the deputies are asked to leave.

The deputies of the nobility and the majority of those of the clergy then leave the room; the deputies of the Third are, as for them, tended and intrigued by the massive presence of the troops. After several minutes of hesitation, the deputy of Aix Mirabeau intervenes and addresses the room: "Sirs, I admit that what you have just heard could be the salvation of the fatherland, if the presents of despotism were not always dangerous. What is this insulting dictatorship? The apparatus of the weapons, the violation of the national temple to order you to be happy! [...] Is Catilina at our doors!" Faced with the uproar caused by this harangue, the grand master of ceremonies Henri-Evrard de Dreux-Brézé then addressed Bailly, dean of the Assembly and the Tiers, to remind him of the king's order. The deputy retorted: "The assembled Nation cannot receive orders". It is then that Mirabeau interferes and, according to the legend, answers him this famous sentence: "Go and tell those who sent you that we are here by the will of the people and that we will leave only by the power of bayonets". Informed of the incident, Louis XVI is said to have blurted out, "They want to stay, well, damn it, let them stay!" A bourgeois and peaceful revolution has thus been accomplished and the king must now choose between accepting the constitutional monarchy or the trial of strength. He seems to be moving towards the first solution while his entourage is more intransigent, in particular his brother the count of Artois who accuses Necker, this liberal banker, of treason and wait-and-see attitude.

Defection from the army

The following day, June 25, the majority of the clergy deputies and 47 deputies of the nobility (including the Duke of Orleans, cousin of the king) joined the Third Estate. Louis XVI tried to give the change and, on June 27, ordered "his faithful clergy and nobility" to join the Third

State; paradoxically, he had three infantry regiments deployed around Versailles and Paris, officially to protect the holding of the Estates General, but in reality in order to be able to disperse the deputies by force if that proved necessary. However, several companies refused to submit to orders and some soldiers threw away their weapons before coming to the gardens of the Palais-Royal to be applauded by the crowd. The Parisian "patriots" followed closely the movements of the army and, when about fifteen insubordinate grenadiers were locked up in the abbey prison of Saint-Germain-des-Prés, 300 people came to free them: "The hussars and dragoons sent to restore order shouted "Long live the Nation!" and refused to charge the crowd.

Louis XVI then mobilized 10 new regiments around Paris. On July 8, Mirabeau asked the king to remove the foreign troops (Swiss and Germans), to which the sovereign retorted that his only goal was to protect the elected officials; to do this, he even proposed to transfer the seat of the National Assembly to Noyon or Soissons.

Dismissal of Necker (July 11, 1789)

The National Assembly, proclaimed on June 17, 1789, took the name of *Constituent* on July 9. During this time, the king dismissed Necker (whose absence from the royal session of June 23 he did not appreciate) and replaced him with the baron de Breteuil, a convinced monarchist.

He called Marshal de Broglie to the post of Marshal General of the King's camps and armies, reinstated to deal with the events.

Taking of the Bastille (July 14, 1789)

The announcement of the dismissal of Necker and the appointment of Breteuil and de Broglie put Paris in turmoil. From that moment on, demonstrations multiplied in Paris; one of them was repressed at the Tuileries, killing one demonstrator.

On July 13, the 407 electors of Paris (who had elected their deputies for the Estates General) met at the Paris City Hall to form a "permanent committee. They founded a militia of 48 000 men framed by French guards and adopted as a sign of recognition the bicolored red and blue cockade, in the colors of the city of Paris (the white, symbol of the nation, was inserted in the tricolored cockade born in the night of July 13 to 14).

On the morning of the 13th, Louis XVI wrote to his younger brother, the Count of Artois: "To resist at this moment would be to expose oneself to lose the monarchy; it would be to lose us all. [I believe more prudent to temporize, to give in to the storm, and to wait for the time, for the awakening of the good people, and for the love of the French for their king".

All the demonstrators had to do was find weapons. On July 14, a crowd estimated at 40,000-50,000 people showed up in front of the Hôtel des Invalides. The officers gathered under the orders of Besenval on the Champ-de-Mars unanimously refused to charge against the demonstrators. Thus the latter freely seized inside the Invalides about 40,000 Charleville rifles, a mortar and half a dozen cannons. All that was missing was powder and bullets, and the idea spread that the fortress of the Bastille was full of them.

At about 10:30 a.m., a delegation of Paris voters went to the governor of the prison, Bernard-René Jordan de Launay, to negotiate the surrender of the requested weapons. After two refusals, Launay blew up 250 barrels of gunpowder; the explosion was mistakenly considered a charge against the attackers. Suddenly, a former sergeant of the Swiss guards surrounded by 61 French guards arrives from the Invalides with the stolen cannons and places them in position to attack the Bastille. The fortress capitulates, the crowd rushes in, freeing the 7 prisoners and seizing the ammunition. The garrison of the Bastille, after having massacred a hundred rioters, is led to the Hôtel de ville while the head of Launay, decapitated on the way, is exposed on a pike. Unaware of the events, Louis XVI ordered too late that the troops stationed around Paris evacuate the capital.

The next day, July 15, the king woke up to learn from the grand master of the wardrobe, François XII de La Rochefoucauld, about the events of the previous day. According to legend, the king asked him: "Is this a revolt?" And the Duke of La Rochefoucauld replied, "No, Sire, it is a revolution."

From that day on, the Revolution was irreversibly set in motion. Louis XVI, who can only choose between civil war and resignation, agrees to capitulate to events.

Also on July 15, the king went to the Assembly to confirm to the deputies that he had ordered the troops to withdraw from the vicinity of Paris. Under the applause of the deputies, he concludes his visit by saying: "I know that one dared to publish that your people were not in safety. Would it be necessary therefore to reassure you on such guilty noises, denied in advance by my known character? Well, it is I who am only one with the Nation which relies on you: help me in this circumstance to ensure the salvation of the State; I wait for it of the National Assembly ". By addressing the *National* Assembly directly, Louis XVI had just officially recognized its existence and legitimacy. Immediately, an important delegation led by Bailly went to the Paris City Hall to announce to the people the king's dispositions and to bring back calm in the capital. In a festive and dancing atmosphere, Bailly is appointed mayor of Paris and La Fayette is elected by the Assembly as commander of the National Guard.

Recall of Necker and adoption of the tricolor cockade by the king (July 16-17, 1789)

On July 16, the king held a council in the presence of the queen and her two brothers. The Count of Artois and Marie-Antoinette asked the king to transfer the court to Metz for more security, but the king, supported by the Count of Provence, kept it in Versailles. He later regretted not having moved away from the epicenter of the Revolution. He also announced in this council that he was going to recall Necker and ordered Artois (whose repressive philosophy he reproached) to leave the kingdom, making the future Charles X one of the very first emigrants of the Revolution.

Necker thus returned to the government with the title of Controller General of Finances. Montmorin was also recalled to Foreign Affairs, Saint-Priest to the King's Household and La Luzerne to the Navy. Necker will soon realize that the power now resides in the National Assembly.

On July 17, Louis XVI set out for Paris to meet his people. Accompanied by a hundred deputies, he chose to go to the Hôtel de Ville, which had become the symbolic center of popular protest. He was received by the new mayor,

Bailly, who addressed him in these terms: "I bring to Your Majesty the keys of his good city of Paris: they are the same that were presented to Henry IV, he had reconquered his people, here the people have reconquered their king. Under the cries of "Long live the Nation!", he had the tricolor cockade affixed to his hat. He then entered the building by passing under the vault formed by the swords of the national guards. It is then that the president of the electoral college, Moreau de Saint-Méry, compliments him: "The throne of the kings is never more solid than when it has for base the love and the fidelity of the people". The king then improvised a small speech during which he declared to approve the nominations of Bailly and La Fayette; showing himself to the crowd which acclaimed him below, he said to Saint-Méry: "My people can always count on my love". Finally, at the request of the lawyer Louis Éthis de Corny, a vote was taken to erect a monument to Louis XVI on the site of the Bastille.

As the historian Bernard Vincent noted in commenting on this reception at the Hôtel de Ville: "With the storming of the Bastille, the supreme power had indeed changed sides.

Great Fear (July 19 - August 6, 1789)

With the National Assembly now ruling the country, the king's intendants left their posts in the provinces. The

French peasantry was very much afraid that the lords, in order to take revenge for the events in Paris, would send "brigands" against the people of the countryside.

Coupled with hunger and fear of the wheat grabbers, the great fear prompted the peasants to create militias throughout France. If they failed to kill the imaginary brigands, the militia members burned castles and massacred counts in particular. The Assembly, hesitant in the face of these exactions, decided to calm the game down. Nevertheless, fear spread to the city of Paris where, on July 22, the State Councillor Joseph François Foullon and his son-in-law Berthier de Sauvigny were massacred on the Place de Grève.

Abolition of privileges (August 4, 1789)

In order to put an end to the instability reigning in the countryside, the dukes of Noailles and Aiguillon launched the idea to the Constituent Assembly of making a clean sweep of all the seigneurial privileges inherited from the medieval period. Thus, during the night session of August 4, 1789, feudal rights, tithes, drudgery, mainmorte and the right of garenne were abolished. The assembly affirms the equality in front of the tax and the employment, abolishes the venality of the charges and all the ecclesiastical, noble and bourgeois advantages.

Although Louis XVI asserted in a letter the next day to Monseigneur du Lau, archbishop of Arles, that he would never give his sanction (understand his agreement) to decrees that would "strip" the clergy and nobility, the Assembly continued to legislate in this direction until August 11. The decrees of application will be taken on March 15 and July 3, 1790.

Declaration of the Rights of Man and the Citizen (August 26, 1789)

The report rendered on July 9 by Jean-Joseph Mounier presented an order of work for the drafting of a Constitution beginning with a declaration of rights. This declaration was to serve, as a preamble, to propose to the universe a text "for all men, for all times, for all countries" and to codify the essential of the spirit of the Enlightenment and of Natural Law. The idea was also to oppose to the royal authority the authority of the individual, the law and the Nation.

On August 21, the Assembly began the final discussion of the text, tabled by La Fayette and inspired by the Declaration of Independence of the United States. The text was adopted article by article, ending on August 26, when the deputies began to examine the text of the Constitution itself.

The Declaration fixes at the same time the prerogatives of the citizen and those of the Nation: the citizen by the equality in front of the law, the respect of the property, the freedom of expression in particular, and the Nation by the sovereignty and the separation of the powers among others. The text is adopted "in the presence and under the auspices of the Supreme Being, an abstract and philosophical god.

The debates, stormy, occur in the middle of 3 categories of deputies who begin to distinguish themselves from each other: the right (*aristocrats*), the supporters of the *status quo* like d'Eprémesnil or the abbot Maury; the center (*Monarchians*) led in particular by Mounier and in favor of an alliance between the king and the third estate; and finally the left (*patriots*), itself composed of a moderate branch in favor of a minimal veto of the king (Barnave, La Fayette, Sieyès) and an extreme branch with still few deputies (Robespierre and Petion in particular).

Royal veto (September 11, 1789)

Following the adoption of the final text of the Declaration of the Rights of Man and of the Citizen on August 26, the Assembly turned to the question of the king's veto. After a few days of debate, which took place in the absence of the main interested party, the deputies voted on September 11, by a very large majority (673 votes against 325), the *suspensive* veto proposed by the patriots. In concrete terms, the king loses the initiative of the laws, and keeps only the right of promulgation and the right of remonstrance. Louis XVI accepted this idea in a spirit of conciliation, thanks to Necker who, having negotiated this option with the patriots, was able to convince the king to accept the right of veto thus voted.

Nevertheless, the deputies conceded the right of veto to the king only if the latter endorsed the decrees of the night of August 4. In a letter of September 18, Louis XVI writes to the deputies that he agrees with the general spirit of the law but that on the other hand important points were not studied, in particular the future of the treaty of Westphalia devoting the feudal rights of the Germanic princes having lands in Alsace. For any answer, the assembly summons the king to promulgate the decrees of August 4 and 11. Outraged, Louis XVI conceded on September 21 that he accepted the "general spirit" of these texts and that he would publish them. Satisfied, the deputies granted on September 22 (by 728 votes against 223) the right of suspensive veto for a duration of six years. At the same time, they voted in the article of the future constitution according to which "the government is monarchical, the executive power is *delegated* to the king to be exercised under his authority by the ministers.

Return of the king to Paris (October 6, 1789)

Despite his return to government, Necker was unable to redress the finances of the kingdom. He therefore resorted to the traditional remedy of borrowing: two loans were launched in August 1789, but the results were poor. Necker therefore went to the Assembly as a last resort to propose an extraordinary contribution that would be levied on all citizens, and which would be equivalent to a quarter of everyone's income; initially reluctant to vote for this heavy tax, the said Assembly adopted it unanimously, convinced by the words that Mirabeau had spoken to him: "Vote for this extraordinary subsidy [...] the hideous bankruptcy is there: it threatens to consume you, your property, your honor [...] and you deliberate!" The lifting of this contribution, however, does not solve the economic difficulties of the country, bread becoming increasingly scarce and unemployment increasingly strong (one of the consequences of the emigration of aristocrats, among whom many employers).

The public opinion is moved by this impasse and, sensitive to the counter-revolutionary thrusts of the court and the king (who is now called *Monsieur Veto*), distrusts more and more the sovereign and his entourage. For example, in the song *La Carmagnole*, probably composed during the day of August 10, 1792:

"Mr. Veto had promised
to be faithful to his country;
but he failed to do so.

Let's not be in the same neighborhood anymore."

This mistrust soon turned into revolt when the people learned that during a dinner given on October 1er at Versailles in honor of the Flanders regiment (which had come to lend a hand in the defense of the court), some officers did not fail to trample on the tricolor cockade and to shout "Down with the Assembly!", all in the presence of Louis XVI and the Queen

The Parisians learn the news, relayed and amplified by the newspapers; Marat and Desmoulins call to arms against this "counter-revolutionary orgy". According to the official registers, only "53 sacks of flour and 500 setiers of wheat" have entered the capital for the last 10 days; in the face of this shortage, it is rumored that wheat is abundantly kept at Versailles and moreover that the king plans to transport the court to Metz. The Parisians therefore wanted to bring back the wheat and to retain the king, even if it meant bringing him back to the capital.

On October 5, a crowd of women invaded the Paris City Hall to express their grievances and to inform that they were going to march to Versailles to speak to the Assembly and to the king himself. Led by the bailiff

Stanislas-Marie Maillard, about 6,000 to 7,000 women, plus a few agitators in disguise, went on foot to Versailles, "armed with rifles, pikes, iron fangs, knives on sticks, preceded by seven or eight drums, three cannons, and a train of powder barrels and cannonballs, seized at the Châtelet.

On hearing the news, the king returned hastily from hunting and the queen took refuge in the cave of the Petit Trianon. Around 4 pm, the procession of women arrived in front of the Assembly; a delegation of about twenty of them was received in the Menus-Plaisirs room, which demanded that the king promulgate the decrees of August 4 and 11 and sign the Declaration of the Rights of Man. A horde of female citizens came into the room, shouting: "Down with the cap! Death to the Austrian! The king's guards to the lantern! "

Louis XVI accepts to receive five of the women of the procession, accompanied by the new president of the Assembly, Jean-Joseph Mounier. The king promised them bread, kissed one of the women (Louison Chabry, 17 years old), who fainted under the emotion. The women came out shouting "Long live the king!" but the crowd shouted treason and threatened to hang them. They promise then to return to the king to obtain more. Louis XVI then gives to Jérôme Champion de Cicé, Garde des Sceaux the written order to bring wheat from Senlis and

Lagny; he also promises to Mounier that he will promulgate the same evening the decrees of August 4 and 11, and that he will also sign the Declaration. Showing himself at last on the balcony at the side of Louison Chabry, he moves the crowd which cheers him then.

Around midnight, La Fayette arrived at the castle at the head of the National Guard and some 15,000 men; he promised the king that he would ensure the external defense of the castle and assured him: "If my blood must flow, let it be for the service of my king. The next morning, after a night spent camping on the Place d'Armes, the crowd witnessed a fight between demonstrators and several bodyguards; the rioters then led the crowd into the castle through the door of the chapel, which had remained strangely open. A real carnage followed, where several guards were massacred and decapitated, their blood staining the bodies of the murderers. The latter seek out the queen's apartments, crying out: "We want to cut off her head, fricassee her heart and her livers, and it won't end there!" Borrowing secret corridors, the king and his family manage to find themselves together under the cries of "The king in Paris!" and "Death to the Austrian!" coming from outside. The queen then said to her husband: "You did not know how to decide to leave when it was still possible; now we are prisoners". Louis XVI then consulted with La Fayette; the latter opened the window leading outside and showed himself to the crowd, who shouted "The king on the balcony! The sovereign then shows himself to the crowd without saying a word, while the crowd cheers and asks him to return to Paris. Voices calling for the queen, La Fayette tells her to come to the window as well: "Madame, this step is absolutely necessary to calm the crowd". The queen complies, moderately acclaimed by the crowd; La Fayette kisses her hand. The king then joined her in the company of his two children and declared to the crowd: "My friends, I will go to Paris with my wife and children. It is to the love of my good and faithful subjects that I entrust the most precious thing I have.

After a 7-hour drive, the procession arrived in Paris, flanked by the National Guard and the freshly cut heads of the morning. Wagons of wheat also accompanied the royal family, so that the crowd declared that it brought back to the capital "the baker, the baker and the little baker". After a formal detour to the Hôtel de Ville, the procession reached the Palais des Tuileries, where the royal family took up residence for the last time; a month later, the Assembly took up residence in the nearby Salle du Manège. On October 8, the deputies Fréteau and Mirabeau proposed to establish the title of King of the French instead of King of France. The Assembly adopted this new title on October 10, and decided on October 12 that the sovereign would not be titled "King of the

Navarrese" nor "King of the Corsicans". The Assembly will formalize these decisions by a decree of November 9. Louis XVI began to use the new title (spelled "King of the Franks") in his letters patent from November 6. On February 16, 1790, the Assembly decreed that its president should ask the king that the seal of the state bear the new title. The new seal is used from February 19, with the wording "Louis XVI by the grace of God and by the constitutional loyalty of the State king of the Franciscans". And the Assembly decides by decree of April 9, 1791, that the title of king of the French will henceforth be engraved on the coins of the kingdom (where always appeared that of king of France and Navarre: *Franciæ et Navarræ rex*). The title is then maintained in the constitution of 1791.

Dechristianization policy and the king's reactions

From the first months following the beginning of the Revolution, the Church and the clergy were the target of the new policy; as the historian Bernard Vincent affirms, "it is this aspect of the Revolution, this relentlessness against the Church, that Louis XVI, not only a man of faith but also deeply convinced of being an emissary of the Almighty, had the most difficulty in admitting. He will never admit it, in spite of the public concessions that day after day his situation imposes him to make ".

One of the first acts of this desire to de-Christianize institutions was the decree of November 2, 1789, by which the Assembly, on the initiative of Talleyrand, decided by 568 votes to 346 that the property of the clergy would be used to make up the national deficit.

On December 19, 1789, the Assembly put into circulation 400 million assignats, a type of Treasury bill, intended to pay off the debts of the State. The value of these assignats was eventually guaranteed by the sale of the clergy's property; nevertheless, the excessive issuance of these bills will result in a strong depreciation, up to 97% of their value.

On February 13, 1790, the Assembly voted to prohibit religious vows and to suppress regular religious orders, except for educational, hospital and charitable institutions. Orders such as the Benedictines, Jesuits and Carmelites were declared illegal. In several cities, violent clashes between royalist Catholics and Protestant revolutionaries took place, such as in Nîmes where, on June 13, 1790, 400 people died.

The Civil Constitution of the Clergy was voted on July 12, 1790, filling Louis XVI himself with dread. Henceforth, the dioceses would be aligned with the newly created departments: there would thus be 83 bishops for 83 dioceses (for 83 departments), and in addition 10 "metropolitan bishops" in place of the existing 18 archbishops. But the reform, decided without consultation with either the clergy or Rome, also foresees that parish priests and bishops will henceforth be elected by citizens, even non-Catholics. Having no more income following the sale of the property of the clergy, the priests will thus be public servants paid by the State but will have, in return, to take an oath of fidelity "to the Nation, to the law and to the king" (article 21). The constitution divided the clergy into two camps: the swearing priests (a slight majority), who were faithful to the constitution and to the oath of fidelity, and the refractory priests, who refused to submit to it. The civil constitution of the clergy and the Declaration of the Rights of Man were condemned by Pope Pius VI in the apostolic brief *Quod aliquantum*, bringing back into the Church some swearing priests. The Assembly took its revenge with the decree of September 11, 1790, attaching the Papal State of Avignon and the Comtat Venaissin to the Kingdom.

On December 26, 1790, Louis XVI resigned himself to ratify the civil constitution of the clergy in its entirety. As he had indicated to his cousin Charles IV of Spain in a letter sent on October 12, 1789, he reluctantly signed these "acts contrary to royal authority" which had been "taken from him by force.

Fête de la Fédération (July 14, 1790)

Two days after the vote of the civil constitution of the clergy, and to celebrate the 1er anniversary of the storming of the Bastille, the Champ-de-Mars is the scene of a large-scale ceremony: the Fête de la Fédération.

Orchestrated by La Fayette on behalf of the *federations* (associations of national guards in Paris and the provinces), the Fête de la Fédération brought together some 400,000 people, including members of parliament, the Duke of Orleans from London, members of the government, including Necker, and the royal family. A mass was presided over by Talleyrand, surrounded by 300 priests in tricolor stole.

Louis XVI takes a solemn oath in these terms: "I, King of the French, swear to the Nation to use the power delegated to me [...] to maintain the Constitution decreed by the National Assembly and accepted by me and to enforce the laws". The queen presents her son to the crowd under the acclamations.

The king is acclaimed throughout the day and Parisians come in the evening to shout under his windows: "Reign, Sire, reign!" Barnave recognized: "If Louis XVI had known how to take advantage of the Federation, we were lost. But the king did not take advantage of the situation: for some historians, the king wanted to avoid a civil war; the other explanation comes from the fact that the king had perhaps already undertaken to leave the country.

Escape and arrest at Varennes (June 20-21, 1791)

Faced with the decay of his power, Louis XVI did not choose to abdicate, believing that the anointing received at his coronation and the secular character of the monarchy prevented him from doing so. Therefore, the king opted to flee the kingdom [ref. needed].

After a kidnapping plan led by the Count of Artois and Calonne, which was impossible to implement, and an assassination attempt of Bailly and La Fayette planned by Favras in 1790, the king built a plan to escape from the kingdom in the direction of Montmédy, where the Marquis de Bouillé was waiting for him, and then to the Belgian provinces of Austria. Historians differ as to the actual purpose of the plan. According to Bernard Vincent, if the king had succeeded in finding refuge in the East, "then that changed everything: a vast coalition could be formed - allying Austria, Prussia, Sweden, Spain and why not England - which would bring the Revolution to its knees, take support from deep in France, reverse the course of history and restore King Louis and the monarchical regime in their immemorial rights. The date of the escape was set for June 20, 1791; the practical arrangements, such as the production of false passports, disguises and transportation, were entrusted to Axel de Fersen, the queen's lover and henceforth the royal family's supporter.

On June 20, around 9 p.m., Fersen brought the sedan that was to be used to transport the royal family to the Porte Saint-Martin. At half past midnight, the king, disguised as a valet, the queen and Madame Elisabeth boarded a hired carriage to join the sedan where the dauphin, his sister and their governess Madame de Tourzel were already seated. The carriage then leaves; Fersen accompanies the royal family to Bondy where he takes leave of them.

On June 21 at 7 o'clock, the valet of room realizes of the disappearance of the king. La Fayette, the National Assembly, and then the whole city of Paris learn the news; it is not known yet if it is a kidnapping or an escape. The king had a handwritten text deposited in the Assembly, the *Declaration of the King, addressed to all the French people when he left Paris*, in which he condemned the Assembly for having made him lose all his powers and urged the French people to return to their king. In fact, in this text written on June 20, he explains that he spared no effort as long as he "could hope to see the rebirth of order and happiness", but when he saw himself "prisoner in his States" after his personal guard had been taken away from him, when the new power deprived him of the right to appoint ambassadors and to declare war, when he was restricted in the exercise of his faith, "it is natural, he says, that he sought safety".

This document was never circulated in its entirety. On the one hand, Louis XVI denounced the Jacobins and their growing hold on French society. On the other hand, he explains his will: a constitutional monarchy with a powerful executive and autonomous from the Assembly. This major historical document, traditionally called "the political testament of Louis XVI" was rediscovered in May 2009. It is in the Museum of Letters and Manuscripts in Paris. The king comments on his feelings about the revolution, criticizing some of its consequences without rejecting important reforms such as the abolition of orders and civil equality.

Meanwhile, the sedan continued eastward, crossing the city of Châlons-sur-Marne four hours behind schedule. Not far from there, at Pont-de-Sommevesle, Choiseul's men were waiting for it; not seeing the sedan arrive in time, they decided to leave.

At 8 o'clock in the evening, the convoy stopped in front of the relay of Sainte-Menehould and then resumed its route. The population wonders about the mysterious carriage, and very quickly the rumor spreads that the fugitives are none other than the king and his family. The postmaster, Jean-Baptiste Drouet, is summoned to the town hall: when he sees a money order bearing the king's image, he recognizes the king as one of the passengers in the convoy. He then set off in pursuit of the sedan with the dragon Guillaume in the direction of Varennes-en-Argonne, towards which the carriage was heading. Taking shortcuts, they arrived before the convoy and managed to warn the authorities only a few minutes before the arrival of the king. The royal family arrived around 10:00 a.m. and ran into a roadblock. The public prosecutor Jean-Baptiste Sauce checked the passports, which seemed to be in order. He was about to let the travelers leave when the judge Jacques Destez, who had lived in Versailles, formally recognized the king. Louis XVI then confessed his true identity; he was unable to convince the population that he was planning to return to Montmédy to settle his family, especially since the postmaster of Châlons arrived at that very moment, bearing a decree from the Assembly ordering the arrest of the fugitives. Choiseul, who managed to reach the king, proposed to the latter to clear the city by force, to which the king replied to wait for the arrival of General Bouillé; but he did not come and his hussars made a pact with the population. The king then confided to the queen: "There is no more king in France".

Informed on the evening of June 22 of the events that took place in Varennes, the Assembly sent three emissaries to meet the royal family: Barnave, Pétion and La Tour-Maubourg. The meeting took place on the evening of June 23 at Boursault. The procession spends the evening in Meaux and takes again the following day the road of Paris, where the Assembly has already decreed the suspension of the king. A huge crowd had gathered along the boulevards to see the royal family's carriage pass; the authorities had put up posters on which it was written: "Whoever applauds the king will be beaten, whoever insults him will be hanged. During the journey, the king kept an exemplary calm as Pétion noted: "It seemed that the king was coming back from a hunting trip [...] he was just as phlegmatic, just as quiet as if nothing had happened [...] I was confounded by what I saw". As for Marie-Antoinette, she noticed in a mirror that her hair had turned white.

The Assembly decided to hear the royal couple on the Varennes affair. Louis XVI only made it known that he had not intended to leave the national territory: "If I had intended to leave the kingdom, I would not have published my memoir the same day I left, but I would have waited until I was outside the borders. On July 16, he was informed that he was cleared and that he would be reinstated as soon as he had approved the new constitution.

For the historian Mona Ozouf, the king's failed flight broke the bond of the indivisibility of the king and France, because, she explains, it "presents to the eyes of all the separation of the king and the nation: the first, like a vulgar emigrant, ran clandestinely to the frontier; the second rejects henceforth as derisory its identification with the body of the king, which no restoration will succeed in reviving any more; by which, well before the killing of the king, it accomplishes the death of the royalty".

Preparation of the Constitution

The republican idea, already on its way, will suddenly accelerate on the occasion of the failed flight of the king. On June 24, 1791, a petition calling for the establishment of a Republic gathered 30,000 signatures in Paris. On June 27, the Jacobins of Montpellier call for the creation of a Republic. Thomas Paine founded at the end of June the club of the *Republican Society*, with more advanced ideas than that of the Jacobins, within which he elaborated a republican manifesto, where he called on the French people to end the monarchy: "The nation can never return its confidence to a man who, unfaithful to his duties, perjures his oaths, hatch a clandestine escape, fraudulently obtains a passport, hides a king of France under the disguise of a servant, directs his course to a border more than suspicious, covered with defectors, and obviously meditates to return to our states only with a force capable of dictating its law to us." This appeal is posted on the walls of the capital and then, on July 1er 1791, on the door of the National Assembly; this initiative does not fail to shock a certain number of deputies, who disassociate themselves from this movement: Pierre-

Victor Malouet spoke of a "violent outrage" against the Constitution and public order, Louis-Simon Martineau demanded the arrest of the authors of the poster, and Robespierre exclaimed: "I have been accused within the Assembly of being a republican. I have been given too much honor, I am not!"

On July 16, the Jacobin Club was torn apart over the question of the republic; the majority wing hostile to a change of regime gathered around La Fayette and created the Club des Feuillants. On July 17, the Club des Cordeliers (led by Danton, Marat and Desmoulins in particular) launched a petition in favor of the republic. The text and the 6,000 signatures are deposited on the altar of the Fatherland erected on the Champ-de-Mars for the 2e Fête de la Fédération on July 14. The Assembly orders the dispersion of the crowd: Bailly orders martial law and La Fayette calls in the National Guard. The troops fired without warning despite the orders received and killed more than 50 demonstrators. This tragic episode, known as the Fusillade du Champ-de-Mars, was to be a turning point in the Revolution, leading immediately to the closing of the Club des Cordeliers, the exile of Danton, the resignation of Bailly as mayor of Paris in the autumn, and the loss of popularity of La Fayette in public opinion.

The Assembly continued drafting the Constitution from August 8 and adopted the text on September 3. Preceded by the Declaration of the Rights of Man, it recognized the inviolability of the king, set aside the Civil Constitution of the Clergy (reduced to the status of ordinary law), maintained the censal vote and provided for the appointment of ministers by the king outside the Assembly. For the rest, most of the power was vested in the Assembly, elected for two years. On the other hand, nothing was provided for in the event of disagreement between the legislative and executive branches: the king could not dissolve the Assembly and the Assembly could not censure the ministers. This text, considered rather conservative, disappointed the left-wing deputies.

Archival sources relating to the members of the Constitutional Guard of Louis XVI are described by the National Archives (France).

Louis XVI took the oath to the new Constitution on September 14. The president of the Assembly, Jacques-Guillaume Thouret (after having sat down) declares to Louis XVI that the crown of France is "the most beautiful crown in the universe", and that the French nation "will always [need] the hereditary monarchy". The king signs the Constitution. It will be then under the safeguard of the deputy Jean-Henry d'Arnaudat (former adviser to the parliament of Navarre), who will sleep with it until the next day. On September 16, the Constitution was published in the *Gazette Nationale*. The Constituent

Assembly met for the last time on September 30, to give way to the Legislative Assembly the following day.

Foreign policy

One of the first areas that will escape the king is that of foreign policy, which he had previously conducted with pride and efficiency.

First of all, Belgium, influenced by the revolutionary rise of France, became independent and the emperor Joseph II was deposed on October 24, 1789, and was immediately replaced by his brother Leopold II. Austria took control of Belgium and the Liège Republic ended on January 12, 1791.

On May 22, 1790, the Assembly took advantage of the Nootka crisis between Spain (France's ally) and Great Britain to decide whether the king or the national representation had the right to declare war. The question was settled that day by the Decree of Declaration of Peace to the World, in which the Assembly decreed that this decision was its own. It states that "The French nation renounces undertaking any war with the aim of making conquests [...] it will never use its forces against the freedom of any people".

On August 27, 1791, Emperor Leopold II and King Frederick William II of Prussia jointly drafted the Declaration of Pillnitz, in which they invited all European sovereigns to "act urgently in case they were ready" to organize reprisals if the French National Assembly did not adopt a constitution in conformity with "the rights of the sovereigns and the welfare of the French nation. The counts of Provence and Artois sent the text to Louis XVI with an open letter urging the king to reject the draft constitution. Louis XVI is distressed by this letter, having addressed himself a secret letter to his brothers where he indicated to them to play the card of the conciliation; he reproaches them their attitude in these terms: "Thus you will show me to the Nation accepting with one hand and soliciting the foreign powers with the other. What virtuous man can estimate such a behavior? "

King of the French and monarchy (1791-1792)

First constitution of France

Louis XVI is maintained as *king of the French* by the new Constitution. He is still king "by the grace of God", but also "by the constitutional law of the State", that is to say not only a sovereign of divine right, but in a way the head, the first representative of the French people. He retained all executive powers, which he exercised by virtue of human law. This constitution also maintained the change of the title of the dauphin to "prince royal" (which had taken place on August 14, 1791).

On September 14, 1791, Louis XVI swore loyalty to the said constitution.

The new Assembly, elected on the basis of censal suffrage, did not include any deputy of the former Constituent Assembly. It includes 745 deputies: 264 registered in the group of Feuillants, 136 in that of Jacobins and 345 Independents.

New economic crisis at the end of 1791

France went through a new crisis at the end of 1791: the popular unrest in the West Indies caused a reduction of sugar and coffee, and thus a rise in their price. The value of assignats deteriorates, the price of wheat increases and the people are hungry.

Diplomatic crises and declaration of war against Austria

On October 30 and November 9, the new Assembly adopted two decrees on emigration: in the first, it asked the Count of Provence to return to France within two months or risk losing his rights to the Regency; in the second, it urged all emigrants to return or risk being accused of "conspiracy against France," punishable by death. The king validated the first decree but vetoed the second twice, on November 11 and December 19. The Assembly later adopted the law of December 28, 1793, which placed at the disposal of the Nation the movable and immovable property confiscated from individuals considered to be enemies of the Revolution, i.e. emigrants and fugitives, refractory priests, deportees and prisoners, those condemned to death, and foreigners from enemy countries.

On January 21, 1792, the Assembly obtained from the king an official warning to Leopold II asking him to denounce the Declaration of Pillnitz. The emperor died on March 1er, without having responded to this appeal, but having taken care a few weeks earlier to sign a treaty of alliance with Prussia. His son François II succeeded him and intended to make the Revolution bend, affirming: "It is time to put France either in the necessity of executing herself, or of making war on us, or of putting us in the right to make it to her". The Girondins suspected the queen of connivance with Austria. Louis XVI then dismissed his moderate ministers and called de Grave to the War as well as a number of Girondins: Roland de la Platière to the Interior, Clavière to the Finances and Dumouriez to Foreign Affairs. It will be "the jacobin ministry". On June 10, Roland warned the king that he had to give his approval to the action of the Assembly: "It is no longer time to back down, there is no longer any way to temporize. [...] Still some delay, and the upset people will see in their king the friend and the accomplice of the conspirators". Louis XVI, faced with this letter made public, which was an insult to the royal dignity, dismissed Roland and the other moderate ministers - Servan and Clavière. As the only proof of his sincerity as King of the French, Louis XVI, under the influence of this ministry, sanctioned on April 4 the legislative decree of March 24, which imposed in the colonies the equality of free whites and free men of color.

An ultimatum was sent to Francis II on March 25, enjoining him to expel the French emigrants from his country, which remained without response. The king therefore agreed, at the request of the Assembly, to declare war on Austria on April 20, 1792. Many people reproached the king for this "double game": if France won, he would emerge stronger from the events; if it lost, he would be able to regain his monarchical powers thanks to the support of the victors.

The Revolution having disorganized the armed forces, the first times were disastrous for France: Marquain's rout on April 29, Rochambeau's resignation, desertion of the Royal-German Regiment in particular. A climate of suspicion was created and the Assembly, distrustful of the street and of the sans-culottes, decided to create a camp of 20,000 federates near Paris; on June 11, the king vetoed the creation of this camp (to avoid a weakening of the protection of the borders) and took advantage of the occasion to reject the decree of May 27 on the deportation of the refractory priests Faced with the protests of Roland de la Platière in particular, Louis XVI made a ministerial reshuffle that did not convince the Assembly.

Day of June 20, 1792

Faced with the rout of the army, the dismissal of the ministers Servan, Roland and Clavière, and the refusal of the sovereign to adopt the decrees on the creation of the federate camp and the deportation of the refractory priests, the Jacobins and Girondins undertook a showdown for June 20, 1792, the anniversary of the oath of the Jeu de paume. Several thousand Parisian demonstrators, led by Santerre, were encouraged to go to the Tuileries Palace to protest against the mismanagement of the war.

Alone, Louis XVI received the rioters. They demanded that the king cancel his vetoes and recall the dismissed ministers. During this long occupation (which lasted from 14 hours to 22 hours), the king did not give in but kept a striking calm. He asserts: "Force will do nothing to me, I am above terror". He even agrees to wear the Phrygian cap and to drink to the health of the people. Pétion leaves to lift the siege, assuring the king: "The people have presented themselves with dignity; the people will leave in the same way; may your Majesty be at peace".

Fall of the monarchy

Faced with Austrian and Prussian advances in the north, the Assembly declared on July 11 that the "Fatherland was in danger. On July 17, a few days after the 3e commemoration of the Fête de la fédération, the provincial federates and their Parisian allies submitted a petition to the Assembly calling for the suspension of the king.

The events will accelerate more on July 25 by the publication of the Manifesto of Brunswick where the duke of Brunswick warns the Parisians that if they do not submit "immediately and unconditionally to their king", Paris will be promised "to a military execution and to a total subversion, and the rebels [...] to the torments which they deserve". The royal couple was then suspected of having inspired the idea of this text. Robespierre asks for the deposition of the king on July 29.

On August 10, around 5 a.m., the sections of the suburbs, as well as the federates from Marseille and Brittany, invaded the Place du Carrousel. The Tuileries Palace was defended by 900 Swiss Guards, their commander, the Marquis de Mandat, having been summoned to the Hôtel de Ville (where a Paris Commune had just been formed) before being assassinated there. The king went down to the courtyard of the palace at 10 o'clock and realized that the building was no longer protected. He decided to seek refuge with his family at the Assembly. Then the insurgents rushed into the palace and massacred all those they met there: Swiss guards, servants, cooks and maids. The castle was looted and the furniture devastated. More than a thousand people were killed during the assault (including 600 Swiss out of 900) and the survivors were later tried and executed.

The insurrectionary Commune obtained from the Assembly the immediate suspension of the king and the convocation of a representative convention. The same evening, the king and his family were transported to the

Couvent des Feuillants where they remained for three days in the greatest destitution.

Transfer of the Royal Family to the Temple House

On August 11, the Assembly elected an executive council of six ministers and set the election of the Convention for early September. It also re-established censorship and asked citizens to denounce suspects. Finally, it asked that the royal family be transferred to the Palais du Luxembourg, but the Commune demanded that it be transferred to the priory hospital of the Temple, under its guard.

It was on August 13 that the royal family was transferred, led by Pétion and escorted by several thousand armed men. For the moment, the family did not occupy the large, unfinished Temple Tower, but the archivist's quarters on three floors: Louis XVI lived on the second floor with his valet Chamilly (who was replaced by Jean-Baptiste Cléry), the queen and her children on the second floor, and Madame Élisabeth in the kitchen on the first floor with Madame de Tourzel. The members of the family could see each other freely but they were closely supervised.

Louis XVI occupied his time between reading, educating the dauphin and praying. Sometimes he played ball with his son and played trictrac with the ladies. The queen also took care of her children's education, teaching history to the dauphin and dictation and music exercises to her daughter.

September Massacres

The day of August 10, 1792 left Paris with a restless climate where the enemies of the Revolution were hunted down. The external news nourish a climate of plot against this one: crossing of the border by the Prussians, siege of Verdun, uprising of Brittany, Vendée and Dauphiné.

The Parisian prisons contained between 3,000 and 10,000 prisoners, consisting of refractory priests, royalist agitators and other suspects. The Commune wanted to finish off the enemies of the Revolution before it was too late. A municipal officer informed the king, who was locked up in the Maison du Temple, that "the people were furious and wanted to take revenge".

For a week, starting on September 2, the most virulent insurgents of the Commune massacred approximately 1,300 prisoners in the following prisons: the Abbey prison, the Carmelite convent, the Salpêtrière prison, the Force prison, the Grand Châtelet prison and the Bicêtre prison.

Victory of Valmy

On September 14, the Prussians crossed the Argonne, but the French armies of Kellerman and Dumouriez (successor of La Fayette who had defected) joined on the 19th. The French army found itself in numerical superiority and had at its disposal a new artillery that the engineer Gribeauval had given it a few years earlier under the impulse of Louis XVI.

The battle began at Valmy on September 20. The Prussians were quickly defeated and took refuge behind their border. The invasion of France was stopped and, as Goethe, who accompanied the Prussian army at the time, said: "From here and from this day a new era in the history of the world begins.

Implementation of the Convention

The Legislative Assembly decided to set up a convention elected following the day of August 10. The elections take place from September 2 to 6 in a context of fear and suspicion due to the Franco-Austrian war and the massacres of September.

At the end of the vote, 749 deputies were elected, including many well-known revolutionaries: Danton, Robespierre, Marat, Saint-Just, Bertrand Barère, Abbé Grégoire, Camille Desmoulins, the Duke of Orleans renamed *Philippe Égalité*, Condorcet, Pétion, Fabre d'Églantine, Jacques-Louis David and Thomas Paine among others. While the voters in Paris voted for the Jacobins, the Girondins won in the provinces.

It is in the context of the victory of Valmy which galvanizes the spirits that the Convention meets for the first time on September 21, 1792, marking from its arrival the abolition of the Monarchy.

SUPPLICE DE LOUIS XVI, PLACE DE LA RÉVOLUTION,
le 21 Janvier 1793 ou 1er Pluviôse An 1er de la République

Abolition of the monarchy and last months (1792-1793)

First measures of the Convention

The National Convention decreed, during its first session on September 21, 1792, that "royalty is abolished in France" and that "Year I of the French Republic" would begin on September 22, 1792. Louis XVI lost all his titles and the revolutionary authorities called him Louis Capet (in reference to Hugues Capet, whose nickname was erroneously considered as a family name). The decrees blocked by the veto of Louis XVI were then applied.

On October 1er, a commission was set up to investigate a possible trial of the king, based in particular on the documents seized at the Tuileries Palace.

Transfer of the royal family to the Temple Tower

On September 29, the king and his valet de chambre Jean-Baptiste Cléry were transferred to an apartment on the second floor of the Temple Tower. He thus left the lodging of the archivist at the priory of the Temple hospital, where he had been living since August 13.

Marie Antoinette, her daughter Madame Royale, Madame Elisabeth and their two maids were transferred to the upper floor of the tower on October 26, in an apartment similar to that of the now former king.

Trial before the Convention

Setting up

The National Convention had already set up a commission on October 1er to investigate the trial. The commission submitted a report on November 6, in which it concluded that *Louis Capet* should be tried "for the crimes he had committed on the throne. Such a trial was now legally possible, since under a republic the inviolability of the king no longer existed.

On November 13, a crucial debate begins about who will conduct the trial. The deputy of the Vendée, Morisson, asserts that the king has already been condemned by having been deposed. Opposite him, some like Saint-Just call for his death, stating in particular that the king is the natural "enemy" of the people, and that he does not need a trial to be executed.

The evidence of the king's guilt was tenuous until November 20, when an iron cabinet was discovered in the

Tuileries, hidden in one of the walls of the king's apartments. According to the Minister of the Interior, Roland de la Platière, the documents found there demonstrated the collusion of the king and queen with the emigrants and foreign powers; he also stated, without further clarification, that some deputies were compromised. Although according to some historians, such as Albert Soboul, the documents reported "do not provide formal proof of the king's collusion with enemy powers," they will nevertheless convince the deputies to indict the king. In a speech on December 3, which has remained famous, Robespierre solemnly advocated the death of the deposed king without delay, declaring that "the people [...] do not pass sentences, they throw lightning; they do not condemn kings, they plunge them back into nothingness [...]. I conclude that the National Convention must declare Louis a traitor to the fatherland, a criminal against humanity, and have him punished as such [...]. Louis must die because the fatherland must live.

After stormy debates, the Convention decided that Louis Capet would indeed be tried, the court being the Convention itself. It confirmed on December 6 that Louis Capet would be "brought to the bar to be interrogated". Saint-Just then saw fit to specify that "it is not [a monarch] that we are going to judge; it is the monarchy [and the] general conspiracy of kings against the people. The next day, Louis XVI and his wife had all their sharp objects confiscated, including razors, scissors, knives and penknives.

Course of action

The trial of the former king, judged as an ordinary citizen and henceforth called *Citizen Capet*, opened on December 11, 1792. From that day on, he was separated from the rest of his family and lived in isolation in an apartment on the second floor of the Temple house, with only his valet, Jean-Baptiste Cléry, for company. His apartment, which was more or less the same as the one in which he lived with his family on the upper floor, measured about 65 m^2 and consisted of four rooms: the anteroom where the guards took turns and in which a copy of the Declaration of the Rights of Man and of the Citizen of 1789 was hung, the king's bedroom, the dining room and the valet's room.

The 1er interrogation takes place on December 11. Around 1 p.m., two personalities came to get him: Pierre-Gaspard Chaumette (prosecutor of the Paris Commune) and Antoine Joseph Santerre (commander of the National Guard). Calling him from now on under the name of Louis Capet, they are retorted by the person concerned: "Capet is not my name, it is the name of one of my ancestors. [I am going to follow you, not to obey the Convention, but because my enemies have the force in hand". Arriving in the full hall of the Manege, the accused was greeted by

Bertrand Barère, the president of the Convention, who asked him to sit down and announced: "Louis, we are going to read you the enunciative act of the offences which are imputed to you." Barère to then take up the charges one by one and ask the king to respond to each of them. The reasons for the charges are numerous: massacres of the Tuileries and the Champ-de-Mars, betrayal of the oath taken at the Feast of the Federation, support of the refractory priests, collusion with the foreign powers, etc. Answering each question calmly and briefly, Louis XVI maintained that he had always acted in accordance with the laws that existed at the time, that he had always opposed the use of violence and that he had disavowed the actions of his brothers. Finally, he denied recognizing his signature on the documents shown to him, and obtained from the deputies the assistance of a lawyer to defend himself. After four hours of interrogation, the king was brought back to the Tower of the Temple and confided to Cléry, his only interlocutor from then on: "I was far from thinking about all the questions that were made to me. And the valet of room to notice that the king "went to bed with much tranquility".

Louis XVI accepted the proposal of three lawyers to defend him: François Denis Tronchet (future editor of the Civil Code), Raymond de Sèze and Malesherbes. However, he refused the help offered by the feminist Olympe de

Gouges. The trial of the king was closely followed by the great foreign powers, in particular Great Britain (whose Prime Minister William Pitt the Younger refused to intervene in favor of the deposed sovereign) and Spain (which informed the Convention that a death sentence on the king would call into question its neutrality with regard to the events of the Revolution).

The interrogations followed one another without yielding anything, each of the parties sticking to their positions. On December 26, de Sèze addressed the deputies in these terms: "I seek judges among you, and I see only accusers. On December 28, Robespierre refutes the idea that the fate of the king should be put into the hands of the people through primary assemblies; he asserts that the French would be manipulated by the aristocrats in this sense: "Who is more talkative, more skilful, more fertile in resources, than the intriguers [...], that is to say, than the rascals of the old and even of the new regime?

The conclusion of the debates fell to Barère on January 4, 1793, in a speech in which he emphasized the unity of the conspiracy, the divisions of the Girondins on the appeal to the people, and finally the absurdity of resorting to it. The resumption of the deliberations was scheduled for the following January 15, when three points would be discussed: the guilt of the king, the appeal to the people, and the punishment to be inflicted. Until then, the king devoted his days to prayer and writing, and on December 25, 1792 he had written his will.

Votes and verdict

The outcome of the trial takes the form of the vote of each deputy on the three questions raised by Barère, each of the elected officials voting individually from the rostrum.

The Convention decides on January 15, 1793 on the first two questions, namely:

- guilt of the king for "conspiracy against public freedom and the general safety of the state": 691 for and 10 abstentions ;
- Appeal to the people to ratify the judgment: 424 against, 287 for, 12 abstentions.

From January 16 at 10:00 am to January 17 at 8:00 pm, the vote on the sentence to be applied will take place, each of the voters will be asked to justify their position:

- 366 votes for immediate death, 34 for death with suspension of execution, 319 votes for detention and banishment, 2 votes for hard labor.

Part of the Assembly asked for a new vote, arguing that some members did not agree with the category in which their vote was classified. On January 17, the new vote took place:

- 361 votes for immediate death, 26 for death subject to examination of the possibility of a stay of execution (Mailhe's amendment), 44 for death with suspension, 290 for other sentences, 5 abstentions.

On January 19, a new roll call took place: "Will the execution of the judgment of Louis Capet be suspended? The vote is finished on January 20 at 2 a.m.:

- 380 votes against the stay of execution, 310 in favor, i.e. 70 majority votes for execution without delay.

Public execution

Louis XVI was guillotined on Monday, January 21, 1793 in Paris, on the Place de la Révolution (now the Place de la Concorde). With his confessor, the abbot Edgeworth de Firmont, the king climbed the scaffold. The knife fell at 10:22 am, under the eyes of five ministers of the provisional executive council.

According to his executioner, he declares during his installation on the scaffold: "People, I die innocent!", then to the executioner Sanson and his assistants "Gentlemen,

I am innocent of all that I am charged with. I wish that my blood could cement the happiness of the French".

In his book *Le Nouveau Paris*, published in 1798, the writer and political essayist Louis-Sébastien Mercier recounts the execution of Louis XVI in these terms: "[...] Is this really the same man that I see jostled by four executioners, forcibly undressed, whose voice is muffled by the drum, garroted to a board, still struggling, and receiving the blow of the guillotine so badly that he had not the neck but the occiput and jaw horribly cut? ".

Death certificate in the civil status of Paris

The death certificate is written on March 18, 1793. The original of the act disappeared during the destruction of the archives of Paris in 1871 but it had been copied by archivists. Here is what the text says: "Monday, March 18, 1793, the second year of the French Republic.
 Death certificate of Louis Capet, last January 21, ten hours and twenty-two minutes of the morning; profession, last King of the French, aged thirty-nine years [sic], native of Versailles, parish of Notre-Dame, domiciled in Paris, tower of the Temple ; married to Marie-Antoinette of Austria, the aforementioned Louis Capet executed on the Place de la Révolution by virtue of the decrees of the National Convention of the fifteenth, sixteenth and nineteenth of the aforementioned month of January, in the presence of 1° Jean-Antoine Lefèvre,

substitute for the sindic public prosecutor of the department of Paris, and Antoine Momoro, both members of the directoire of the aforementioned department and commissioners in this part of the general council of the same department; 2° François-Pierre Salais and François-Germain Isabeau, commissioners appointed by the provisional executive council, to attend the said execution and to draw up a report of it, which they did; and 3° Jacques Claude Bernard and Jacques Roux, both commissioners of the municipality of Paris, appointed by it to attend this execution; having regard to the report of the said execution of the said day, January 21 last, signed Grouville, secretary of the provisional executive council, sent to the public officers of the municipality of Paris this day, on the request which they had previously made to the ministry of justice, the said report deposited at the Archives of the civil status;

Pierre-Jacques Legrand, public officer (signed) Le Grand ".

Grave

He was buried in the Madeleine cemetery, rue d'Anjou-Saint-Honoré, in a common grave and covered with quicklime. On January 18 and 19, 1815, Louis XVIII had his remains and those of Marie-Antoinette exhumed and buried in the Saint-Denis basilica on January 21. In addition, he had the Chapelle expiatoire built in their memory on the site of the Madeleine cemetery.

Tributes

- Abbé Berlier pronounces a funeral oration from Jersey on January 21, 1794.

- Every year since 1815, catholic masses are celebrated in memory of Louis XVI, in many towns of France, on January 21, the anniversary of his execution.

- Two American cities are named Louisville in honor of Louis XVI whose soldiers supported the Americans against Great Britain during the War of Independence. They are Louisville, Kentucky, founded in 1778, and Louisville, Georgia, founded in 1786. A statue of the king, donated in 1967 by the sister city of Montpellier, stands in front of the Louisville Metro Hall in Kentucky.

- The Place de l'Obélisque (or Place Louis XVI) in Port-Vendres in the Pyrenees-Orientales, hosts an obelisk which is the first monument built in France to the glory of Louis XVI during his lifetime. To mark the birth of Port-Vendres with a symbol, Louis XVI allowed the province to erect this monument to his glory in 1780/1786 thanks to the king's architects Charles De Wailly and Louis-Hiver Pons. The obelisk is not topped by a statue of the monarch but is decorated with four bronze bas-reliefs on its base representing "La Marine relevée" (The Raised Navy), "La Servitude abolie" (The Abolition of Servitude), "La Liberté de commerce" (Freedom of Commerce) and "L'Indépendance de l'Amérique" (The Independence of America). Stripped of its ornaments in 1793, the obelisk was only restored to its bas-reliefs in 1956.

- Five statues of the king are still present in France:

    o The statue of Nantes at the top of the Louis-XVI column. The column was erected in 1790 and was only topped by a statue of the king as a Roman emperor in 1823. The work of the sculptor Dominique Molknecht was replaced by a copy of the Nantes sculptor Georges Perraud in 1926.

    o The statue of Le Loroux-Bottereau in Loire-Atlantique. Located in front of the Saint-Jean-Baptiste church, the original 1823 work by Dominique Molknecht is currently in the town's tourist office; a copy has taken its place in front of the church.

- The statue of Plouasne in the Côtes-d'Armor. Located in the gardens of the castle of Caradeuc, the work was commissioned in 1826 by the town hall to Dominique Molknecht to be placed in the niche of the town hall; but being completed after the Revolution of 1830, it was relegated to the museum of Fine Arts of Rennes for 120 years. In 1950, Alain de Kernier, the owner of the Château de Caradeuc, obtained the loan of this statue of the king from the Rennes City Hall, and placed it at the end of a short alleyway now known as the Louis XVI alleyway.

- The statue of Sorèze in the Tarn. It has been located in the gardens of the town's abbey-school since 1857; it was commissioned by Father Henri-Dominique Lacordaire on the occasion of the school's secular feast, to honor the founder of the Royal Military School of Sorèze in 1776.

- The statue of Nant in Aveyron. It can be seen at the tourist office, but its head is missing, after having been decapitated three times. The king had martyrdom palms on his head.

- The square Louis-XVI in Paris with the expiatory chapel built in memory of Louis XVI and Marie-Antoinette in 1826.

- In Cherbourg-en-Cotentin, a rue Louis-XVI has honored the memory of the sovereign and all that he accomplished for the city since 1839.

- On May 3, 1826, on the Place de la Concorde, Charles X laid the first stone of the monument to the memory of Louis XVI. But the statue was never built. Its base will be used for the Luxor obelisk erected in 1836. The current Concorde bridge was named after Louis XVI before the Revolution.

- A colossal bronze statue of Louis XVI, 5.83 meters high, was nevertheless sculpted by Nicolas Raggi. It was kept in the Museum of Fine Arts in Bordeaux. Commissioned in 1825, it was cast in 1828 and destroyed in 1941. The destruction was photographed.

- The Louis XVI Circle is a literary and artistic society in Nantes. Founded in 1760, the "Chambre littéraire de la ville de Nantes" took the name of cercle Louis XVI in 1878. It is currently housed in the Hotel Montaudouin.

- December 20, 1765 - May 10, 1774: Dauphin of France *(at the death of his father Louis, he became the heir to the throne of France; the Dauphin of France did not have the predicate of royal highness at that time)*;

- May 10, 1774 - November 6, 1789: *His Majesty* the King of France and Navarre *(on the death of his grandfather Louis XV)*;

    - May 10, 1774 - January 21, 1793: *His Majesty* the King of France and Navarre *(he is still considered king by the royalists and by the countries that do not recognize the French Republic)*;

- November 6, 1789 - August 10, 1792: *His Majesty* the King of the French *(from November 6, 1789, Louis XVI took the title of King of the French, which the Assembly had adopted on October 10, and which it made official by decree on November 9; the Constitution, which came into force on September 14, 1791, maintained this new title)*.

Descendants

On May 16, 1770, the Dauphin Louis Auguste married the Archduchess Marie-Antoinette of Austria, the youngest daughter of François de Lorraine, Grand Duke of Tuscany and Sovereign Emperor of the Holy Roman Empire and his wife Marie-Thérèse, Archduchess of Austria, Duchess of Milan, Queen of Bohemia and Hungary. This union is the concretization of an alliance aiming at improving the relations between the House of Bourbon (France, Spain, Parma, Naples and Sicily) and the House of Habsburg-Lorraine (Austria, Bohemia, Hungary, Tuscany). The couple, although 14 and 15 years old at the time, did not actually consummate their marriage until seven years later, and four children were born of their union, but they had no descendants:

- Marie-Thérèse of France (December 19, 1778 - October 19, 1851), known as "Madame Royale", who married in 1799 her first cousin the Duke of Angouleme (1775-1844);
- Louis-Joseph-Xavier-François of France (October 22, 1781 - June 4, 1789), first dauphin;
- Louis Charles de France (March 27, 1785 - June 8, 1795), duke of Normandy, second dauphin and future Louis XVII, nicknamed "the Child of the Temple" during his captivity;
- Sophie-Béatrice de France (July 9, 1786 - June 19, 1787) known as "Madame Sophie
- Ernestine Lambriquet ;

- Jean Amilcar;
- Jeanne Louise Victoire

Gallery of portraits
- 1922: *Marie Antoinette, das Leben einer Königin* by Rudolf Meinert with Viktor Schwannicke
- 1923: *L'Enfant-Roi* by Jean Kemm with Louis Sance
- 1924: *Janice Meredith* by E. Mason Hopper with Edwin Argus
- 1925 : *Madame Sans-Gène* by Léonce Perret with Louis Sance
- 1927 : *Napoleon* by Abel Gance with Jack Rye
- 1930: *Captain of the Guard* by John S. Robertson; Louis XVI is played by Stuart Holmes
- 1931 :
    - *Danton* by Hans Behrendt with Ernst Stahl-Nachbaur
    - *Die Marquise von Pompadour* by Willi Wolff with Hans Rameau
    - *Un caprice de la Pompadour* by Willi Wolff and Joe Hamman with Jacques Christiany
- 1934: *Madame du Barry* by William Dieterle with Maynard Holmes
- 1938 :

- *Marie Antoinette* by Woodbridge S. Van Dyke; Louis XVI is played by Robert Morley
    - *La Marseillaise* by Jean Renoir; Louis XVI is played by Pierre Renoir
    - *Let's go up the Champs-Élysées* by Sacha Guitry; Louis XVI is played by Jean Hébey
- 1945: *The Fighting Guardsman* by Henry Levin with Lloyd Corrigan
- 1946: *L'affaire du collier de la reine* (*The Queen's Necklace Affair*) by Marcel L'Herbier; Louis XVI is played by Jean Hébey
- 1954 : *Si Versailles m'était conté...* by Sacha Guitry; Louis XVI is played by Gilbert Bokanowski
- 1955 :
    - *Marie-Antoinette, Queen of France* by Jean Delannoy with Jacques Morel
    - *Napoleon* by Sacha Guitry; Louis XVI is played by Gilbert Bokanowski
- 1956 :
    - *Si Paris nous était conté* by Sacha Guitry; Louis XVI is played by Gilbert Bokanowski
    - *Marie-Antoinette Queen of France* by Jean Delannoy; Louis XVI is played by Jacques Morel
- 1959: *John Paul Jones, Master of the Seas* by John Farrow; Louis XVI is played by Jean-Pierre Aumont

- 1960: *La Fayette* by Jean Dréville; Louis XVI is played by Albert Rémy
- 1970: *Start the revolution without us* by Bud Yorkin; Louis XVI is played by Hugh Griffith
- 1975 : *Marie-Antoinette* by Guy Lefranc; Louis XVI is played by François Dyrek
- 1978 : *On efface tout* by Pascal Vidal; Louis XVI is played by Jacques Ardouin
- 1979: *La Nuit de l'été (Summer Night)* by Jean-Claude Brialy; Louis XVI is played by Henri Tisot
- 1981: *The Mad History of the World* by Mel Brooks; Louis XVI is played by Mel Brooks
- 1982: *La Nuit de Varennes (The Night of Varennes)* by Ettore Scola; Louis XVI is played by Michel Piccoli
- 1984 : *Liberté, Égalité, Choucroute* by Jean Yanne; Louis XVI is played by Michel Serrault
- 1988 :
  - *Chouans !* by Philippe de Broca; Louis XVI is played by Jean Zaluski
  - *Le Gerfaut* by Marion Sarraut; Louis XVI is played by Vincent Solignac
- 1989 :
  - *The Summer of the Revolution* by Lazare Iglesis; Louis XVI is played by Bruno Cremer

- - *The French Revolution* by Richard T. Heffron and Robert Enrico; Louis XVI is played by Jean-François Balmer
  - *Louis XVI, programmed king* by Patrick Le Gall, a documentary on the monarch's career until the Revolution and his image after his death
- 1995: *Jefferson à Paris* by James Ivory; Louis XVI is played by Michael Lonsdale
- 1996 :
  - *Ridicule* by Patrice Leconte; Louis XVI is played by Urbain Cancelier
  - *Beaumarchais, l'insolent* by Édouard Molinaro; Louis XVI is played by Dominique Besnehard
- 2005 : *Marie-Antoinette* miniseries by Alain Brunard with Michel Fau
- 2006: *Marie-Antoinette* by Sofia Coppola; Louis XVI is played by Jason Schwartzman
- 2008 : *Nicolas Le Floch* by Jean-François Parot with Louis Barraud
- 2009: *That day, everything changed: The Escape of Louis XVI*, by Arnaud Sélignac; Louis XVI is played by Antoine Gouy
- 2011 : *Louis XVI, l'homme qui ne voulait pas être roi* (*Louis XVI, the man who didn't want to be

king) by Thierry Binisti; Louis XVI is played by Thierry Binisti
- 2012: *Les Adieux à la reine (Farewell to the Queen)* by Benoît Jacquot; Louis XVI is played by Xavier Beauvois
- 2018: *Un peuple et son roi* by Pierre Schoeller; Louis XVI is played by Laurent Lafitte

Other books by United Library

https://campsite.bio/unitedlibrary

Printed in the USA
CPSIA information can be obtained
at www.ICGtesting.com
LVHW011456281123
765014LV00009B/964